THE Career Game Plan

Preparing Student-Athletes to Compete and Win in the World of Work

SHAUN TYRANCE, PH.D.
&
NYAKA NIILAMPTI, PH.D.

IN COLLABORATION WITH CAREER PARTNERS, INC.

Foreword

Congratulations! If you have made it this far, you are already among the elite. You are a member of the collective group of student-athletes who made up fewer than 3% of the 21 million students attending colleges and universities in America last year (Fast Facts, 2015). I understand what it has taken for you to get here. I was once where you are now. And now I am on the other side, the work side, waiting for you to join my world after graduation.

Have you thought about how you will introduce yourself to the workforce after you graduate? How will you effectively communicate your value to a future employer? How will you hone your skills and market your talents to impress the many interested employers looking for you after your college playing days are over? If you begin to prepare now, you will enjoy a distinct advantage over your non-athlete peers. Your sports career will serve you well in your professional career, and despite what you may think, we in the work world are looking for you. The Career Game Plan will show you how to leverage the work you have been doing your whole life and translate your capabilities to the business community. This book will also help you identify gaps and eliminate weaknesses, while gaining clear understanding of how to play the career game. I challenge you to approach this opportunity with the same passion and focus that has led to your successful athletic career. If you can impress us as you have your coaches and peers by translating your on field talents to the work world, you will find yourself in high demand.

Growing up in suburban Boston, I was a sports fanatic. I played six different sports competitively (from baseball to track) as a kid and another two (golf and tennis) for fun. My family and I constantly juggled my transportation needs, uniform washing, meals on the run, homework in the car, etc. for my events. Sound familiar? By the time my family relocated to Atlanta for the start of my freshman year of high school, I had whittled my competitive sports down to just three.

I also played summer baseball and had an accompanying 30 hour per week job. I didn't go on "Spring Break." I played in tournaments. I didn't spend August at the lake or the beach. I spent it participating in three-a-days in football pads in the sweltering Georgia heat.

By my freshman Spring semester at Colgate University, following surgery for a shoulder injury that essentially ended my football career, I was down to just one sport: baseball. Though my skills were peaking, my passion did not wane, and I kept playing for the camaraderie, for the competition, and for the love of the game. But I knew it would be over soon, and I began to focus on life after college and life after competitive sports. And probably like many of you, I was not exactly sure where to begin.

Fortunately for you, this book will be where you begin, and it just may be the most important book you will read during your entire college career. My good friend and former college quarterback Dr. Shaun Tyrance and his team of experts have compiled an amazing resource to help you proactively manage your transition from college life to work life, and ultimately lead you to a career that will provide you financial resources and intellectual satisfaction. Your authors have created a toolbox that will help you systematically assess your abilities and interests, organize your accomplishments, resolve weaknesses, set goals, and prepare to compete on your post-collegiate playing field.

Have you ever looked around at your fellow students in one of your classes, or in the library, or at an evening, social function and thought to yourself, "these folks have no idea how much effort and time I put into to playing my sport in addition to all my other responsibilities?" In fairness, athletes aren't the only ones taking on additional pressures at school. There are musicians who practice six hours a day and members of the debate team who travel to competitions while learning material about which they will never be formally tested, among many others. Yet just with the examples above, students like you, who are able to distinguish themselves in managing the rigorous curricular and extracurricular balance, will graduate with a distinct and recognizable advantage over students with fewer demands. Your dedication, while perhaps overlooked by your non-athlete peers, will assuredly not be overlooked by your future employers.

In fact, you are already successful in so many of the areas that will ultimately help you distinguish yourself in the workplace: you have mental and physical discipline, you are a successful time manager, you demonstrate leadership, you work successfully within a team, you understand how to compete, and you exercise good sportsmanship. This book will help you package the skills you have been developing your whole life, while providing you a new set of tools to help you translate your current abilities into future opportunities after college.

Just for a moment, think back to your junior and senior years of high school when many of you were deeply engaged in the athletic recruiting process. You collected news clippings, compiled personal statistics, and edited highlight reels of your performance on the field. You recruited coaches, friends, and players to validate your abilities and help convince your favorite schools that you were capable of contributing to their respective sports programs. You may have even visited college campuses and interviewed with coaching staffs and various team members.

What was the purpose of all this? It was to package your skills with the purpose of successfully selling yourself and your abilities to prospective schools and coaches. You had to realistically assess your skills, build your resume, network with your playing peers and supporters, identify schools and athletic programs that fit your goals, interview with coaches and players, and ultimately close the deal. So, in some respects, you have done this kind of search before.

With this book, we take it up a notch and formalize the process to greatly increase your prospects for success. The Career Game Plan will walk you through each of the steps above, and many more as you work through the 14 modules. This time, the approach will be tailored towards helping you succeed in work after college while building a successful career over the longer run. The key for a successful work life, just as with a successful sports life, is preparation. This playbook will prepare you for the biggest and most important opportunity of your life.

"Help Me Help You..."
—Jerry McGuire

Even for those of you unfamiliar with the classic, sports-business movie in which a hot-shot sports agent played by Tom Cruise begs his high-flying, wide receiver client played by Cuba Gooding Jr. to "Help me Help You," the message is paramount — the more you put in, the more you get out. The same qualities that have driven your success on the playing field will drive your success in your career.

Today, I run an investment management firm. My career has included positions with a professional sports organization, a Wall Street investment bank, and a boutique hedge fund before co-founding Kingfisher Capital in 2009.

Every game has rules and if you don't know the rules, you cannot play the game effectively. The work world has rules too, and you better learn how to play the game before you step onto the field. The Career Game Plan will teach you the rules and prepare you for success. If you invest in your future by learning the playbook, you will be amazed at your results now and over time. The Career Game Plan will position you to succeed and really help you win.

Business owners, corporate recruiters, and other professionals are looking for people just like you; people who know how to compete. You are valued in the marketplace. Seize this moment and change the trajectory of you future. It is not enough just to earn your degree, you must do more than that. And it is not enough just to get a good job, you must reinvent yourself throughout your life while keeping your skills current and relevant. The world after intercollegiate sports is just as competitive as the one you are in now. Learn the playbook to compete and win at the next level.

Alexander B. Miles
Managing Partner & Chief Investment Officer
Kingfisher Capital

Career Spotlight

DEVON FRANCOIS is currently a 7th Grade math teacher at Jefferson RISE Charter School. He graduated from Alcorn State University with a Bachelor of Arts in Health and Recreation, and he played safety for the ASU football team.

Contents

MODULE 1

Overview of Career Development

The intent of *The Career Game Plan* is to introduce you, the student-athlete, to the tools you will need in order to manage your transition from the life of a college student-athlete into the rapidly changing and complex working world. Why is *The Career Game Plan* program important? Because, according to the NCAA, while there are more than 460,000 NCAA student-athletes, fewer than 2% will go pro in their sports (Probability of Playing, 2015). Therefore, it is imperative that every student-athlete prepare for life after college. Unfortunately, given the demands that competing at the collegiate level places on your time, energy, and attention — often approaching up to 40 hours a week for athletics alone — it remains extremely difficult to take advantage of this unique opportunity to engage in career planning and exploration during your college career.

> 31% of former athletes did little to no career planning as undergraduates

The goal of this program is to coach you through the career development process and give you the tools necessary to develop a realistic plan for a career after college (and college sports). This plan will be rooted primarily in your own interests, goals, personality, experiences, and skills, both in and out of the world of sport. This program will help you prepare for and then pursue a variety of vocational options that fit your interests and skills. *The Career Game Plan* is important to all students, even those who are considering graduate school. Many students choose graduate school because they are stressed or feel overwhelmed by the change in lifestyle that comes with entering the world of work. The better prepared you are, the less stress you will experience around starting your career. It should be noted that most graduate and professional schools prefer that you have two to three years post undergraduate experience before attending.

As noted, this program is written specifically for you — the 98% of student-athletes who will spend an incredible amount of time while on campus in the pursuit of athletic excellence, but will do something else once your eligibility runs out. We know with certainty that, over the course of your college athletic career, you will be learning and practicing the kinds of transferable skills that are in demand in today's workforce and will serve you well throughout your professional career. For example, teamwork, leadership, discipline, time management, perseverance, risk-taking, and rebounding from failure are all skills organizations look for in their employees. Despite having these and many other abilities and advantages in your toolkit, you will nonetheless find yourself in another competition upon graduation. You will be competing for a rewarding, well-paying, and satisfying job. Your competition will be other college graduates, often from totally different departments, majors, and universities, and who have completely different experiences and backgrounds. Although your competition for these jobs will have vocational goals similar to yours, very few, if any, of them, will have engaged in the 40 hour weekly commitment required in college athletics. Instead, your competition may have held part-time or full-time jobs, summer internships, or found other ways to make their resumes and credentials more appealing to the job market.

"Be realistic, but know you can accomplish what you are determined to accomplish. Being a student-athlete with success in the classroom and on the fields is viewed favorably by employers. You can have a full "college experience" that includes athletics, academic excellence, and extracurricular involvement, but you must learn to balance all the demands effectively. If you can do that well, employers will place you at the top of their list."

—Dentist and Former
Division I Football Player

Our goal through this program is to level the playing field and give you, the collegiate student-athlete, the tools necessary to successfully compete in the job market. We will coach you to master both the concepts and the actual skills associated with winning at the game of career management.

In many ways, this responsibility for taking charge of and continuously managing your own career is a relatively new concept. Until recently, the career planning process really wasn't a big problem. Companies used to hire people, put them to work in entry-level jobs, sometimes at a competitive salary, promote them as appropriate opportunities surfaced, and otherwise watch over them while they worked for the company. Often, in those days, people stayed at their jobs for their entire careers. After you worked for that company for 30 years, they'd throw you a nice retirement dinner, and off you would go to the golf course, into volunteer activities, or into some other form of retirement, with financial security for life.

No longer, though, is this the case. According to 2015 data, the average worker has 11.7 jobs between the ages 18 and 48, and nearly half of these jobs were held from ages 18-24 (Number of Jobs, 2015). As the world of work continues to change, the responsibility for marketing and selling yourself in the job market is a set of life skills that few understand — but these days, everyone needs. This program is intended to introduce you to the very specific skills, behaviors, and insights necessary to not only get a good job after graduation, but also help you understand and execute the practice of managing your own career throughout your working days. With this program, we hope to serve as another one of your coaches — your *career* coach.

Career Game Plan — Three Key Concepts

In sports, before you ever take the field or court, your coaches usually outline a solid game plan to execute for success. Similarly, in order to prepare yourself for the lifelong game of managing your own career, you'll need to understand and act upon the intersection between the three key concepts that will be the basis for all of the activities included in this program. They are:

1. **YOUR QUALIFICATIONS:** As simple as this sounds, first and foremost, you will need to be qualified and able to perform specific kinds of work if you want to get hired — and get paid! Some of your qualifications will come to you in the form of your education (major, classroom, and project work) and internships. And some will come as a result of your athletic endeavors in the form of your demonstrated leadership, perseverance, and ability to learn from your experiences and your coaches. We'll be reminding you throughout this program that you will need to continue to add specific qualifications to your portfolio of skills as your college years progress. You'll certainly gain some of the necessary skills through athletics, but you will not acquire all the skills that you'll need for the working world on the playing field or in the gym. The job you seek after college has to provide you with rewards — financial and otherwise — that are reasonable and in line with your efforts and expectations. However, you'll need to be qualified to perform the work you're hired to do, whether through degrees, certifications, licenses, or hands-on experience. In other words, there has to be a match between what the job market requires and your resume, background, training, and experiences. You will have to be the one who takes responsibility for that. *The Career Game Plan* will help you begin to identify many of the skills you've already developed, and will guide you toward gaining additional skills while on campus that will contribute to your

success in landing employment opportunities after graduation and throughout your career. Similar to your sports performance, the sure way to bring your "A" game from a career perspective is to be prepared. This text will give you the skill set you need to present your best self in your job search process.

2. **THE MARKETPLACE:** The marketplace of jobs and careers has its own rules and rate of change. In order to be effective in managing your career, you will need to learn how to keep up with the trends that will affect various fields of work. Here's an illustration: looking back to the job market of the past, there were once hundreds of thousands of solid "middle class" jobs in assembly line manufacturing settings. Men and women (many without formal education or degrees) worked side-by-side "on the line" at automobile or appliance plants, for example. These were considered good jobs for many, as they paid solid wages (especially with overtime), and a single wage earner could easily support a family with such a job as recently as the 1970's.

Today, however, robotics are in the process of replacing a lot of those manufacturing jobs. And at the same time, the job market is creating and supporting new jobs, such as for industrial-electrical technicians who are building those robots. So, while many of those former "line workers" are still at the plant, they are now being paid to program those robots, using programmable logic control software. On the other hand, this new marketplace is finding it a lot harder (but not impossible!) to replace your nurse, teacher, or speech therapist, for example.

The point of these examples is that you are going to have to learn how to see into the future a little bit, so that you can begin to identify what jobs the market will need in the years ahead. For a job to exist, and to command a competitive salary, there has to be a market, a customer, a consumer, or an end user for the work, just like there has to be a paying ticket buyer to support college and professional sports. Fortunately, there are sources that provide this kind of information out there to help you with these thorny research questions, and we'll expose you to many of them throughout the course of this program.

3. **YOUR PERSONALITY:** Beyond understanding that a "good" job is one that you can do well (see #1 above), and that is supported in a competitive workforce (see #2 above), you should recognize that the work you pursue should allow you to be yourself while you're doing it. The

demands of the work should be aligned with your own unique personality characteristics, personal and professional interests, and personal value system. We will help you explore these seemingly intangible, yet very important issues as well. As a part of this program, we'll help you begin to uncover the unique strengths, skills, and interests that contribute to who you are. You will utilize assessment instruments that are specifically designed to help you better understand yourself and to gain a greater awareness of what satisfies you in the work that you choose to pursue after graduation.

How *The Career Game Plan* Works

In this program, we have broken the complex topics you've just read about into manageable segments. Each module will introduce you more fully to each specific career development topic and will guide you through a very hands-on set of exercises designed to help you put each of the concepts together and into practice. At the end of this program, you will have a well-thought-out and fully executable career exploration plan and strategy. Each step of the process is presented in a specific sequence, and each module puts another building block in place that will culminate for you in a market-ready career management toolkit. Here's how we've broken down the topics for you:

In **MODULE 1**, where we are right now, we present an overview of career development as well as an assessment of your knowledge to date. **MODULE 2**, "Tools of the Trade," will introduce you to the five key tools that make up this toolkit, so you can begin to see more clearly the overall path we've set forth for this career journey of yours. You'll get an overview of the importance of a thorough career assessment, the elements of a well-crafted resume, an overview of the value of learning to research today's job market and the tools to pull it off, as well as an introduction to the importance of developing a comprehensive job search strategy. Finally, we'll cover the process of how to acquire and negotiate job offers through successful interviewing strategies.

In **MODULE 3**, you will begin the actual Career Assessment process by exploring the most widely used career interest survey in the country, the Strong Interest Inventory. This will help you begin to chart a path toward a career choice. We continue with assessment work in **MODULE 4** by guiding you through a process to help you identify the kinds of transferable skills that your athletic and academic experiences have given you. This work will pay double dividends, as you will return to this module later in the program when you use these results to lay the groundwork for building a competitive and market-ready resume.

MODULE 5 is designed to help you begin the process of researching the job market. A good job market analysis will inform you about what jobs are growing or declining in the marketplace, and what skills and education will be needed for you to land a job in that field. You will also learn how to research salary ranges and other key facts about potential career options. We will continue this experience of assessment in MODULE 6 by having you take the Myers Briggs Type Indicator (MBTI), the world's most administered personality assessment instrument. The MBTI will allow you to gain a better understanding of your personality, so you may consider how your personality could and should impact the types of jobs you target.

The Career Game Plan devotes two full modules to resume development and design (Modules 7 and 13). In MODULE 7, you will get an overview of the role resumes play in today's electronic job search universe. You'll also learn about the formatting choices you may need to make when you are ready to enter the job market, and you'll begin the actual resume writing process. We'll continue to build on, and wrap up, the assessment component of this program in Module 8 by having you consider your work-based values. With the assessment instruments that are included in this program, you will gain the kinds of insights into your personality and interests that very few of your future competitors have the opportunity to gain.

In MODULE 9, the program explores the range of options available to you as you begin the process of finding and applying for advertised job openings. We'll cover how to identify and use various websites and job boards, including commercial sites and company home pages. We'll continue with this exploration in MODULE 10, where we give you a road map to begin tackling the task of networking for job search purposes. There is a lot of research out there to suggest that as many as two-thirds of all jobs are landed though this particular aspect of the job search process. We'll give you the tools necessary to navigate this challenging terrain. We also address the broad range of issues associated with using social media to follow employers, gain market information, and get connected to the right people.

Modules 11 and 12 are devoted to the topic of interviewing. We'll cover the basics of preparing for and conducting an interview in MODULE 11, and then move on to helping you master the nuances of Behavioral Interviewing in MODULE 12. Behavioral Interviewing is a specific type of interview style that much of the employment community has adopted to guide their interviewing processes. We'll teach you how that interviewing strategy works from the employer's perspective, and get you ready for your first interview.

In **MODULE 13**, a deeper dive into the nuances of writing a market-ready resume is explored. This module layers in more and more resume design/writing activities that you have completed over the course of the program. You will find yourself building, module-by-module, an outstanding resume that accurately reflects your skills and career interests. We'll also spend some time on cover letters, providing samples for your use. Then we wrap up this program in **MODULE 14** by helping you actually close the deal. We'll cover the steps involved after that first job offer actually comes in, how to evaluate, negotiate, accept, or decline the offer.

> *"Start preparing for getting your first job as early as possible. In college I never thought much about what information should go on a resume, how to sell myself in an interview, or how I should dress when going on interviews. I started learning all of this after I had graduated, and I was looking for jobs. I made some mistakes that I would not have if I had prepared better over the course of my entire college career."*
>
> —Physical Therapist and Former Division III Women's Golfer

In each module you will find quotes from former college athletes who have successfully transitioned into the workforce. We also provide survey data results from a study that we conducted with former student-athletes to learn about their career development needs when they were college athletes. In order for you to put each of the career development concepts into practice, every module has a set of exercises and activities that will provide you with practical, hands-on experience, allowing you to develop your skills in each area. Throughout this program, you will be asked a number of questions about yourself, your interests, and your values. You will need to consider each of these questions seriously and respond as honestly as you can at this point in your life; the results of this exploration will be most helpful if they are a true reflection of you.

As you can see, we have tried to cover every base in introducing you to the complex game of career management. We're convinced that this curriculum should be as much of a focus as you give to your academic and athletic preparation for gradation, and we encourage you to participate fully in each module. It's now more competitive than ever out there in the world of work, and you must have the tools and a solid game plan to be successful. The good news is this: we already know that you — the college student-athlete — loves a challenge, knows how to compete, and loves to win.

EXERCISE

RATIONALE: At the very core of *The Career Game Plan*, and built into all the associated modules and assignments is the assumption that those who take a systematic, step-by-step approach to career exploration and development will ultimately win in the "world of work." The first step to such a process is to figure out where you are now, assess where you need to go from here, and to begin to chart a path to help you get there. The following checklist is simply designed to give you a preliminary look at where you are now in this process, to give you a better understanding of what we will be presenting in the modules to come, to help you assess what progress you might have already made, and finally, to underscore where you'll need to concentrate your efforts over the course of this program.

EXERCISE 1.1: Career Development Needs Assessment

DIRECTIONS: Looking back on the career development activities that you have engaged in to date, please circle Yes (**Y**) or No (**N**) to the questions below.

Y   N   Have you ever undergone a thorough assessment of your personality, values, and interests from a vocational perspective?

Y   N   Have you ever undergone a thorough assessment of your abilities, skills, and accomplishments from a vocational perspective?

Y   N   Have you identified or begun to explore a list of specific jobs, job families, or areas of concentration?

Y   N   Can you list two to four specific job titles that are associated with any of the academic majors that you are considering?

Y   N   Do you have a draft of a professional resume?

Y   N   Do you know how resume management software works, and what formats are best suited for electronic job applications?

Y   N   Have you begun to make a list of key contacts, friends, and supporters who can help you with your upcoming career explorations?

Y   N   Have you ever visited the "career" website page of a major employer?

Y   N   Have you ever had an interview of any kind?

Y   N   Do you know the 10 most common interview questions?

Y   N   Do you know the most effective way to answer Behavioral Interviewing questions?

Y   N   Do you know how to research a potential employer?

Y   N   Are you aware of the salary ranges that are associated with specific jobs or job families that are appealing to you?

Y   N   Can you identify services that are available to you on campus that will support your career development?

Y   N   Can you identify the basic components of a job offer (other than job salary and benefits)?

Y   N   Have you ever negotiated a job offer?

Y   N   Have you ever written basic job search correspondence (cover letters, networking approach letters, interview follow-up, etc.)?

MODULE 2

The Career Management Process — Tools of the Trade

To baseball players, the concept of hitting is pretty straightforward: see the ball, hit the ball. Understanding that concept alone is rarely enough to produce a .300 hitter. What else is needed? You need the actual tools and plenty of practice to be successful. Good hitters know how to use the right tools: the right size/weight bat, the right cleats, the best batting gloves, and they spend plenty of time in the batting cage. This program teaches you to master the right tools for the world of work, so you can successfully identify the kind of vocation that is best suited to your personality. One that is truly interesting and engaging to you, and is consistent with your most closely held values.

45% of former athletes had little to no knowledge of what was expected of them in the workplace as undergraduates.

Landing the kind of job that will make you glad to hear the alarm on Monday morning is the best kind of trophy you can take home from the competition of finding the right job and career. Here's an overview of the five tools we'll be putting into play:

1. **CAREER ASSESSMENT:** Almost all career exploration processes begin with an in-depth assessment. In this program, we will expose you to three different assessment instruments. First, we'll look at the most widely used "interest inventory" in career development today, the Strong Interest Inventory. This will help you begin to identify, or, in some cases narrow down, the actual jobs or job families that are supported in a competitive labor market and appeal to you. We'll use these results later as the basis for learning and practicing some additional skills

and techniques related to ongoing career exploration and research. Later on, we'll add two more assessment instruments: the Myers Briggs Type Indicator (MBTI), the leading measure of personality characteristics in use today. We will wrap up our battery of assessment with a Values Inventory, which will help you identify some of your more closely held personal values that will also impact work (for example, family, lifestyle, and recognition, etc.).

2. **RESUME DESIGN AND DEVELOPMENT:** A resume, at its most basic, summarizes the education, employment history, and experience that is relevant to your ability to land an interview for a particular job. Yet, in today's world of resume management software and key word search technology (more on that later!), you'll need to know not only how to compose an up-to-date and relevant resume, but also how to tailor your resume to fit the specific jobs and/or organizations you want to work for. You'll need to know the kinds of resumes that are in use today, what to include and not include, and what formats, layouts, and content will work best for your particular career interests. Early attention (before you even need a resume) to the resume development process will also be crucial in helping you to start thinking about the specific kinds of experience that should be on your resume. You can then use these college years to seek out and participate in those kinds of activities.

3. **RESEARCHING THE JOB MARKET:** To become an effective career manager, you'll also need to be able to research the job market for career fields that interest to you and to identify organizations that require your unique skills and abilities. Consider this: such jobs as application developers, data miners, and social media managers didn't even exist 10 years ago, while other jobs that did exist in the past are no longer supported in the workforce at all. Thus, you'll need to know which jobs will be sustained in the job market of the future, how to research such issues as the growth (or decline) rates for specific occupations, the typical wages and benefits for certain jobs, and what kinds of credentials, licenses, certifications, or degrees are required for entry into certain jobs. When you start to interview, you'll also quickly find that your ability to be successful in that particular competition is tied to your ability to conduct research. This is research that is necessary to clearly understand that company's current challenges, who they are competing with, and what products they are selling — or not. In short, much like when writing a research paper, you'll need to examine the job market in order to be competitive in the world of work.

4. **JOB SEARCH STRATEGY:** The actual practice of uncovering and applying successfully for jobs is changing rapidly as well, and you'll need a solid understanding of the processes hiring managers use today to find and hire employees. There are well over 100,000 sites on which you can post a resume on the internet today, while employers are simultaneously using their own home pages to post jobs and accept applications. Social media, including LinkedIn, Facebook, and Twitter, are being used more and more in the hiring process these days. Which is better? Why? These are the questions that *The Career Game Plan* will explore as you move through this program. The business models and practices of recruiters — individuals working for the hiring company who are responsible for identifying potential candidates — are also rapidly changing. Meanwhile, good old-fashioned networking, or leveraging those friendships and relationships that you've developed and maintained throughout your life, is still is the single most effective pathway to employment. All of these tools and strategies should be incorporated into one overarching search strategy, and we'll show you how to do that.

> 65% of former athletes stated that they did not have a job search strategy or plan as an undergraduate.

5. **INTERVIEWING AND CLOSING OFFERS:** Everything you will have learned and practiced up until now will be for nothing if, once you get in the employer's door, you can't sell yourself and get that job offer. You'll need to know what kinds of interviewing programs, strategies, and approaches are in use today, and to know how to answer some of those tough questions that you may not yet be ready to deal with. You'll need to know how to prepare for interviews, how to answer typical and difficult questions, and how to close out and follow-up after interviews. Evaluating potential job offers can also be difficult, and approaching any negotiations that may come up without jeopardizing the offer also requires a delicate touch. *The Career Game Plan* will be your step-by-step guide for managing this entire process.

Summary

Not too long ago, you were making a choice about which college to attend. Whether or not you were heavily recruited out of high school, you still had to figure out a few things: What do I want to gain from the college experience? Where do I want to spend the next four years, and what coaching staff do I want to play with? What skills will I develop when I get there? How will this choice help or hurt my future? In the blink of an eye, it'll be time for you to start that process over again. This time, you'll be leaving school and heading into the world of work. The good news for you is that, just as when you were deciding about college, you'll have access to some good coaching. In this case, though, it will be career coaching. You will begin now to understand, design, and execute career plans that will make the transition off of campus and into the world of work as seamless and as rewarding as possible. Like sports, however, you're still going to have to put in the work.

We're going to put a lot of information, resources, and tools in front of you. We'll teach you how the game is played, and what tools and skills you'll need to be able to excel at the game. We'll help you with resumes, interviewing, researching the job market, and even help you think more clearly about your career plans for the future. And again, similar to your athletic endeavors, that combination of great coaching and your individual efforts will put you in the best possible position for success!

> *"Student-athletes should think about their careers more and be more pro-active in understanding the job market. When you think about potential jobs, ask yourself: 1) Can I realistically make enough money to support myself doing this the day after graduation? 2) Will I enjoy doing this job for the 3-5 years? 3) What organizations have these jobs? I recommend that students create a job related goal during their freshman or sophomore year and use the summers to build towards that goal with internships, etc."*
>
> —IT ANALYST AND FORMER DIVISION II WOMENS FIELD HOCKEY PLAYER

Career Spotlight

MARCY MCCLANAHAN is currently a Plant Manager for Trane, a brand of Ingersoll Rand. She graduated from Wake Forest University with a Bachelor's of Arts degree in Sociology, and played point guard for the women's basketball team.

EXERCISE

RATIONALE: When young student-athletes are first challenged to think about where they might fit in within the world of work, many have a really solid and firsthand understanding of only a very few jobs. You may have had a good look at the life of teachers, of coaches, and of your parents' jobs, for example, and you may have held a part-time job or two. Yet, there is a wealth of information about all kinds of jobs to be uncovered from those who have actually been in the workplace for many years. This exercise — where you'll interview two different people about their work — is intended to introduce you to one of the joys of career counseling: the chance to listen carefully as people share with you how they really feel about their work. We promise you'll enjoy this one.

EXERCISE 2.1: Two Interviews

DIRECTIONS: Using the questionnaires below, identify and interview two different people who fit the following criteria:

- Employed outside the field of athletics
- Has a job that you are interested in pursuing
- Has a job that requires a college degree
- Has held the role for more than 3 years
- Seems to genuinely enjoy his/her work

INTERVIEW 1

1. Name:

   _____

2. Occupation/Job Title:

   _____

3. Company/Organization Name:

   _____

4. Years in the profession:

   _____

5. Brief Job Description (2-3 sentences):

   _____

   _____

   _____

   _____

6. 2-3 Key Daily Activities:

   _____

   _____

   _____

   _____

7. What key skills are required for this job?

    _____

    _____

    _____

8. What credentials/degrees/licenses/training are required?

    _____

    _____

    _____

9. What are entry level positions for this type of work?

    _____

    _____

    _____

10. What would entry level salaries be for this type of work?

    _____

    _____

    _____

11. What does he/she like the most about this type of work?

    _____

    _____

    _____

12. What advice would this person give to someone considering this line of work?

_____

_____

_____

Post-Interview Impressions:

_____

_____

_____

_____

_____

_____

INTERVIEW 2

1. Name:

_____

2. Occupation/Job Title:

_____

3. Company/Organization Name:

_____

4. Years in the profession:

_____

5. Brief Job Description (2-3 sentences):

    _____

    _____

    _____

6. 2-3 Key Daily Activities:

    _____

    _____

    _____

7. What key skills are required for this job?

    _____

    _____

    _____

8. What credentials/degrees/licenses/training are required?

    _____

    _____

    _____

9. What are entry level positions for this type of work?

    _____

    _____

    _____

10. What would entry level salaries be for this type of work?

_____

_____

_____

11. What does he/she like the most about this type of work?

_____

_____

_____

12. What advice would this person give to someone considering this line of work?

_____

_____

_____

Post-Interview Impressions:

_____

_____

_____

_____

MODULE 3

The Strong Interest Inventory

One of the best ways to feel confident that you'll actually be happy to jump out of bed and head off to work is to know that you're going to be interested in the work you'll be doing when you get there. Although this seems like a pretty simple concept, there are studies that suggest that as many as 70% of today's American workers don't like their jobs (State of the, 2015). Of course, there are number of reasons for this, but certainly we can assume that one of them is that the work they do is simply not aligned with their interests and personality. Yet, as career coaches, we know that those people who are most satisfied with their career choices are those that have identified a solid fit between their interests and the requirements of their work.

As a college athlete, you've experienced firsthand how your personality and interests have contributed to your ability to enjoy your sport and to be successful in competition. If you're a swimmer, for example, you may have noticed that not all of your teammates or opponents have the same competitive drive to push through that last 50 meters, or an interest in taking the time to study film or learn new techniques that can make the difference between first and second place.

25% of former athletes rarely to never considered looking for a job that aligned with their interests as undergraduates.

You may have also noticed that there are swimmers who have enjoyed similar coaching support, access to similar practice facilities, and have posted outstanding qualifying times that still didn't make it to the winner's podium. Often, the difference between those who make it to this level and those who don't, as most sport psychologists and experienced coaches will tell you, is rarely in the physical tools of the athlete, but in the intangibles: the personality, the values, and the interests that motivate each athlete.

It's no different in the world of work. To enjoy it, to get good at it, even to "make the team" in the first place, you are going to have to find a job that aligns with your interests and strengths. Whether you're trying to decide what courses to take, what major to declare, or what kind of work to pursue, it's important to get all the help you can.

Why a Career Interest Inventory

We have found that, if you ask a lot of children "what they want to be when they grow up," you'll start to see a pattern. They'll scratch their heads for a moment or two, and then come up with a handful of predictable responses: teacher, fireman, doctor, lawyer, or something related to what their parents do for a living. Of course, this makes sense when you realize that there are over 840 different job categories supported in the US job market (Standard Occupational Classification, 2015). College students don't often say they want to be a Field Test Analyst or a Healthcare Monitor Technician, although these are perfectly good jobs that are plentiful in the job market. So, how do you figure out what kind of work you want to pursue, when you don't even know what kind of work is out there?

This limited view of the job market is often even more pronounced in the world of athletics. Typical answers among college athletes to the "what do you want to be when your grow up" question are very often a lot like what we heard from the other young people, but with an athletic focus: professional athlete, coach, athletic director, trainer, strength coach, tickets sales, NCAA administrator, and sport psychologist seem to come up often. While these are a great list of potential career choices, you can see that this list too is limited by what athletes have been exposed to since they began in serious competition. A career interest inventory is a first step in the process of beginning to look outside of your own personal experiences and world view, and allows you to gain an insight into the vast world of work.

Linking Your Interests to Job Titles

Whether or not you're an athlete, it's hard for young people to determine what career path to pursue, simply because they are unfamiliar with the range of career options available. It turns out that while you may be pretty good at telling us some of the activities that you like to do and which activities you are good at, you may lack a clear idea of how these skills and interests align with different career possibilities. This is where the interest inventories come in, as they can provide you with a starting point in your search for a career that you just might end up loving.

The Strong Interest Inventory (SII) is an online assessment that poses a wide range of questions, and uses your answers to statistically compare your likes, dislikes, favorite activities, and personality with the responses of people who are already working in specific careers. With the SII, you answer a series of simple questions such as whether you would enjoy writing a poem, solving a mathematical problem, teaching a child to read, or building a new house for the poor in the inner city. It is important to remember that the SII is not asking you — and it isn't trying to assess — whether you think you can actually DO any of these things. It is not a test or measure of skill, but rather an evaluation of your natural interests. It doesn't make any effort to measure or report on whether you possess the skills to perform any of these activities or even the ability to learn how to do them.

The Strong Interest Inventory is simply an assessment of what you might LIKE to do, not what you can do. It is designed to match up your current interest in various occupations, subject areas, activities, and leisure activities, with the scores and profiles of people who are already working in and enjoying those same specific jobs or job families. While the algorithms are obviously complicated, the bottom line is this: if you answer questions on the SII in the same ways or patterns that Engineers who like their jobs do, then you'll get a score that says you might want to consider Engineering as an occupation.

So, after you take the assessment and you get your report, you'll see right away some very specific job families and job titles that might be a good match for you. Their value to you at this phase of your career journey is in their ability to suggest broad families of jobs or occupational niches for your research or consideration. So, if your interest inventory results suggest a particular job family or vocational direction, you'll now have plenty of time to take an introductory class in one or more of these areas. Biology for those with an interest in Medicine/ Allied Health, for example, or Political Science for those with a preliminary interest in Law. You might also use this information to help you select classes next semester, or select topics for papers in English Composition or Business Writing. Using the results of the SII in this way will give you a focused, but low-risk opportunity to take a few different occupational areas of interest out on a test drive.

"Choose a career path that you are passionate about that fits your interests, rather than choosing it for ease or other factors. If you end up in a career that you don't enjoy, you'll be looking to switch jobs in no time."
—MARKETING MANAGER AND FORMER DIVISION I BASEBALL PLAYER

How Your Results are Organized

Your scores and results will come in a computer-generated report that will be organized chiefly around six "General Occupational Themes" (GOT). These six themes are broad vocational interest areas that represent the personality types originally devised by psychologist John Holland almost 100 years ago. Holland believed that all people, and the places they work, fall into one (or more) of these six types. As mentioned, where you fall within these six types is based entirely on your interests and approaches to life situations as measured on the assessment. Your GOT code will come in the form of a rank order of your highest of these 6 scores. You'll see that the acronym for the six themes is RIASEC (Realistic, Investigative, Artistic, Social, Enterprising, and Conventional), so your code will be a combination of these letters, like RES or SEC, for example. Here are some traits and characteristics of each one:

People who score highly on the Realistic typically:
- See themselves as practical, mechanical, and realistic
- Like and value animals, tools, or machines
- Have good skills in working with tools, mechanical, or electrical drawings, machines, or plants and animals
- Generally avoid social activities such as teaching, healing, and informing others

People who score highly on the Investigative typically:
- Like to study and solve math or science problems and often avoid leading, selling, or persuading people
- Are good at understanding and solving science and math problems
- Value science
- See themselves as precise, scientific, and intellectual

People who score highly on the Artistic typically:
- Like to do creative activities like art, drama, crafts, dance, music, or creative writing and generally avoid highly ordered or repetitive activities
- Have good artistic abilities in areas such as creative writing, drama, crafts, music, or art
- Value the creative arts in areas such as drama, music, art, or the works of creative writers
- See themselves as expressive, original, and independent

People who score highly on the Social typically:

- Like to do things to help people, such as teaching, nursing, or giving first aid, providing information and generally avoid using machines, tools, or animals to achieve a goal
- Are good at teaching, counseling, nursing, or giving information
- Value helping people and solving social problems
- See themselves as helpful, friendly, and trustworthy

People who score highly on the Enterprising typically:

- Like to lead and persuade people and sell things and ideas, and generally avoid activities that require careful observation and scientific, analytical thinking
- Are good at leading people and selling things or ideas
- Value success in politics, leadership, or business
- See themselves as energetic, ambitious, and sociable

People who score highly on the Conventional typically:

- Like to work with numbers, records, or machines in a set, orderly way, and generally avoid ambiguous, unstructured activities
- Are good at working with written records and numbers in a systematic, orderly way
- Value success in business
- See himself or herself as orderly and good at following a set plan

Along with a ranking and description of your scores on the six General Occupational Themes (GOT), you will also see additional information about various interests, work activities, potential skills, and values associated with these themes. Again, your responses will be statistically compared to those of other people who work in and enjoy similar roles or settings. These additional scores include:

- 30 Basic Interest Scales (BIS), with indications of your relative interest in subsets of the GOT's, such as art, science, and public speaking.
- Five Personal Style Scales: learning, working, leadership, risk-taking, and team orientation.
- And, perhaps most importantly, you'll also receive a ranking of scores on 244 Occupational Scales (OS), which indicate the similarity between your interests as measured on the Strong Interest Inventory and those of people working in each of 122 actual occupations.

Your results will include some very specific ideas about how — and where — you might begin to do some preliminary research to further explore the SII's suggestions. We have supplemented the information in your report with a few worksheets to help you begin to build some specific links between your interests and a handful of specific careers that match your individual test results.

Summary

The Strong Interest Inventory (SII) is the most respected and widely used instrument for career exploration and planning in the world. It is based on the idea that people are more satisfied and productive when they work in jobs that they find interesting, and when they work with people whose interests are similar to their own. In the SII, a person's interests are compared to thousands of individuals with similar interests who report being happy in their jobs.

The greatest value the SII offers to you is to help you more clearly draw a straight line from your interests and personality to actual names of job titles, job families, and career paths that you may enjoy. With a preliminary list of jobs that might be of interest, you can begin the process of researching the job market more fully and building out your credentials and resume in a specific direction while you're on campus.

As you review your own SII results and work through the assignments in this section, here are a few thoughts to keep in mind:

1. The Strong Interest Inventory will definitely tell you something about yourself and about your relationship with the world of work. This information, when looked at carefully, will help you make better and more informed decisions about some issues that should be important to you right now, such as: what kinds of classes to take, what majors to pursue, what occupations to explore, and what kinds of internships you may look into as you progress through your college experience.

2. The results from the SII will provide you with a vehicle to focus the discussions you should be having with others as your college career progresses. You'll find that there are a lot of concerned and interested people out there who can, and will, help guide you through the maze that is the world of work. These include counselors, teachers, advisers, parents, mentors, coaches, and potential employers. Sharing these results with others and asking for their feedback are excellent ways to engage them in serious conversations about your career planning.

3. Specifically regarding the Occupational Scales section and results, your selection of two to four careers for further exploration and research is critical to the process of learning how to explore and pursue career options. Although your choices will likely change over time, it is important at this stage of your development to be able to further research and explore any career choice that may come your way in the years ahead. Selecting a few that at least stand the test of the SII's statistical strengths will provide you with a solid starting point for your career exploration.

Career Spotlight

JASON GARROW is currently the Vice President, Business Development for WME | IMG Golf. He has an undergraduate Bachelor of Arts degree in Business Administration from Augustana College and a Master of Science degree in Sport Management from the University of Massachusetts at Amherst. Jason was a four-year member of Augustana's men's basketball team, was a 2-time All-Conference selection, a 3-time Academic All-Conference selection and recipient of an NCAA Post-Graduate Scholarship. In 2006, he became a member of the Augustana College Athletic Hall of Fame.

EXERCISE

RATIONALE: Your results on the Strong Interest Inventory are based on the concept that if people like their jobs, and you share the same interests as them, then you'll likely find that kind of work enjoyable as well. The worksheet below is simply intended to capture the key points from this report that you will want to retain and think about. Later on, you'll be able to use this worksheet to more easily integrate these results, and your reaction to them, into the additional assessment tools you'll be exposed to throughout the course of this program.

EXERCISE 3.1: **Strong Interest Inventory**

DIRECTIONS: After completing the Strong Interest Inventory, summarize your profile results in this section and highlight key interests that might have an impact on your career exploration.

Highest Themes:

_____

Theme Code:

_____

Top 5 Interest Areas

1. _____

2. _____

3. _____

4. _____

5. _____

Areas of Least Interest

1. _____
2. _____
3. _____
4. _____
5. _____

Top 10 Strong Occupations

1. _____
2. _____
3. _____
4. _____
5. _____
6. _____
7. _____
8. _____
9. _____
10. _____

Occupations of Dissimilar Interest

1. _____

2. _____

3. _____

4. _____

5. _____

Personal Style Scales Preferences

1. _____

2. _____

3. _____

4. _____

5. _____

MODULE 4

Understanding & Identifying Your Transferable Skills

n order to better understand the concept of transferable skills, consider the following **HYPOTHETICAL** scenarios:

"Last season, my overall free throw percentage was 84%. However, it went up to 91% in the last month of the season, during conference play, I was actually 100% from the line in the last two minute of our games. This demonstrates two things: the first is that I have the ability to learn from experience and get better with practice, and the other is that I am very calm under pressure, and can be counted on to perform at my best in key and critical moments. This has certainly been true in my basketball career, and I am confident that the same will be true in my working life."

"In my freshman year, I was called "out" in a close play at home plate to end the third inning against our conference rival. I was sure that I was safe, and I argued with the umpire until I got thrown out of the game. Because I was the only left- handed hitter in the top half of the line-up, I took a key bat out of our coach's hand early in the game. We ended up losing that softball game partly because of my selfish act in the third inning. From that day until graduation, for over 100 more games, I never got thrown out again. What I learned from that experience was to put the team first, and to control my emotions

in a public setting. That lesson helped my softball career a lot, and has carried over into my approach to the world of work as well.

These athletes just demonstrated two lessons that will transfer directly into their ability to master the complexities of the working world after graduation. First, they have taken the time and energy to actually think through how their experiences have allowed them to develop skills that are transferable from athletics into the world of work. Secondly, they have developed the ability to talk about these skills to people who will make decisions about whether to hire them after graduation. Unless you can successfully identify and communicate your skills to a potential employer, the odds are against you in getting the jobs for which you are applying.

> *"Today, student-athletes should think earlier about what long term career planning looks like and how to understand what is required in a job. The job market is ultra-competitive, and it will be very important for athletes to build a transferrable skill set that they can market to potential employers"*
> —Accountant and Former Division II Women Golfer

Skills: What are They, and What are Mine?

A skill is something you can do right now and something that you are good at doing. It could come naturally to you or be something you have learned through education, experience, or training. It is these skills, along with your ability to identify and talk about them easily, that employers are actually buying from you when they hire you into a job. These skills tell employers that you have the necessary background, education, credentials, degrees, or hands- on experience to do a good job for them in a work setting. Unless you have spent time assessing yourself, you will have difficulty identifying and defining these skills, which makes it hard to sell yourself to a potential employer. Finally, when you begin to uncover the requirements for the careers that are of interest to you, you will be able to identify those skills that you haven't yet acquired. Those skills that you lack are the best starting point for identifying the activities and experiences you'll want to pursue — both on and off the playing field — while you're still in school. Your goal should be to attain all of the skills necessary for the careers you wish to strive for upon graduation.

> 20% of former athletes indicate that they could not articulate what job related skills they learned from participating in sports as an undergraduate.

Skills are often also called abilities, strengths, or even talents. You can group your skills into categories are as follows:

- **QUALIFICATIONS AND TRAINING:** This would include degrees, licenses, certifications, or other ways that you can demonstrate by academic or similar types of accomplishments that you meet or exceed the formal requirements for a specific job. These might include a state nursing license, a Microsoft certification in certain hardware installation techniques, or a teaching degree and certification.

- **JOB-SPECIFIC (OR JOB-RELATED) SKILLS:** These are examples of accomplishments where you have actually performed a specific type of work. These would include actually installing an HVAC system in your own home or building a computer from a kit yourself, for example.

- **GENERALIST/TRANSFERABLE SKILLS:** Like our examples at the outset of this module, these are skills that are more general in nature, which can transfer easily among a number of work (or athletic) settings. Being able to work effectively in a team setting, or to learn from one's mistakes, are examples that fit this category. These skills are most valuable during the hiring process when you can demonstrate that your skills are greater than other candidates, and thus set you apart from the competition. For example, some people with highly technical skills (e.g., computer programmers, actuaries, web designers) have a reputation for not being the best at communicating with others or managing interpersonal relationships. When you do have that "value- added" skill or trait, you become a candidate with a competitive edge.

Identifying Skills — Start with Accomplishments

One of the most effective ways of both identifying and demonstrating your skills and strengths is by making a list of your specific accomplishments. By describing how you have solved a problem, made a situation better, or managed a difficult set of circumstances, you are both uncovering, and then providing detailed evidence of your successes. These past wins will serve as your next employer's best possible predictor of your ability to solve problems or make things better for their company when they hire you.

To get started on this process, please answer the following set of questions to help you recall five specific events in your past that fit the definitions/descriptions below. As you work through these questions, concentrate on trying to identify those accomplishments that you can actually measure or that have specific, measurable, or quantifiable results, such as "received a 95%," or "contributed $4,050 to the local United Way." Also, try to use different kinds of examples, so that you are covering both your athletic accomplishments and those from other settings. In the job market, you'll certainly want to be able to emphasize both.

Use examples from internships, classes, and school projects, activities, athletic participation, community service, hobbies, and work experience — anything really — to highlight your past experience and behavior. You can cite special accomplishments, whether personal or professional, such as scoring the winning touchdown, being elected president of your Greek organization, winning a prize for your artwork, surfing a big wave, or raising money for charity. Again, wherever possible, quantify your results. Numbers always impress employers. Here are a few questions to jog your memory regarding your past accomplishments:

- What clubs and campus jobs have you held, including titles, duties, and dates of service?
- What internships and summer jobs have you held, including titles, duties, and dates of service?
- What scholarships or research grants have you been awarded, including an estimate of their monetary value?
- How many and what kind of meetings you have facilitated and for what size groups?
- How many partnerships have you initiated, and what were the positive outcomes of these relationships?
- How many and what kind of events have you managed, and for how many attendees?
- How many public speaking engagements have you given, for what size audiences, and on what topics?
- What kind of awards or special recognition have you won, including the names of awards, and for what achievements?
- What courses have you taken, and what were your grades?
- What team projects have you worked on in your classes, and what was your specific role?
- Where and when has your writing been published?
- When have you accomplished a lot despite having little or no resources?
- When have you solved a difficult problem?
- Can you recall a moment when you accomplished something for the first time?
- Have you developed, created, designed, or invented something new?
- Have you ever supervised, managed or trained others?
- Have you ever identified problem(s) or recommended solutions that others did not see?

- Have you ever developed or implemented a new system or procedure?
- Can you remember what you were doing when you felt the happiest or most confident?
- Can you recall times when you had to overcome obstacles?
- Can you recall times when you had to learn a new skill?
- Have you supervised, managed, or led a group(s)?

As you begin to recall these accomplishments, we'll ask you first to select and list five of them by name or title. Then, using the worksheets provided, detail the steps you went through to actually pull them off. Finally, you'll be guided through a process that will help you identify the specific "skills" you used in the process. These will be exactly the kinds of skills that employers are looking for every day in a new hire. Here's how it works: We know that employers spend a lot of time identifying the kinds of skills they want their employees to bring to the job. Many of their questions and concerns are designed to uncover which applicants possess the specific skills they want. What they're really looking for is some kind of proof that you can do the kinds of things they need done in their organization. It is not convincing enough to tell the employer that you're "a good team player" even if you are and even if that's what they're looking for. To prove it to the employer, you'll need to provide more detail of when and how you've used this skill, along with a positive outcome. You're going to have to be able to tell short stories. What you're trying to accomplish here is to be able to easily list and organize your accomplishments for them, to identify the skills it took to pull them off, and then to match these stories to the kinds of expectations that employers are typically looking for in new hires. When you can pull this off, writing resumes and nailing interviews will be much easier than you think.

Summary

In sports, coaches spend a lot of time learning about your skills. They learn your skills so they can accomplish their goals as leaders and managers in competitive situations. They know who to put in the lineup, under what circumstances, and what kind of performance they can expect from their players in game situations.

The same is true of employers in the world of work. As in sports, employers try to evaluate their potential employee's skills, recruit the ones they think have the talent to be successful, and then make "playing time" decisions based on their assessment of how these employees will perform. In the world of work, there's no game film, so employers and hiring managers have to make decisions based on their perception of your potential, and on what they think you will be able to deliver in "game" situations. To get hired in the work force, you need to take the responsibility for evaluating your own accomplishments and skills and then sell your potential to perform at that level to the hiring company. That's why it is important that you do the following:

- Recall and think through those accomplishments in your life that have set you and your performance apart from the crowd
- Assess and think through the specific skills these accomplishments demonstrate to others
- Learn how to talk about both these accomplishments and the skills they represent to others in an articulate and comfortable way
- Evaluate what skills you currently DON'T possess that could stand in the way of you achieving your career goals now, while you're still in school and have the opportunity to add more

Career Spotlight

LEAH LEVENTHAL is currently a Social Worker with A Child's Place. She graduated from The University of North Carolina at Charlotte with a Bachelor's of Social Work, and played for the women's volleyball team. She received her Master's of Social Work from the University of South Carolina.

EXERCISES

RATIONALE: In order to write powerful resumes and perform well in interviews, you'll need the ability to identify and list your skills, but you'll also need to be able to easily and comfortably communicate these skills to others. Knowing your skills, how they transfer specifically into the world of work, and possessing the ability to talk through these skills with others is critical to job search success. Whether this is in resume writing, networking, or interviewing situations. The three exercises below are designed to take you through a systematic process of identifying the accomplishments you are proud of. You will work through each of them in a way that will enable you to talk about them easily with others and help you identify those specific skills you used in each of these accomplishments that are directly transferable to the world of work.

EXERCISE 4.1: **Building Your Accomplishments List**

DIRECTIONS: By name or title only, list 5 key accomplishments from your background.

EXAMPLE:

Accomplishment #1: Led the team to the state championship
Accomplishment #2: Raised $11,000 for the local YMCA
Accomplishment #3: Earned a 3.8 GPA during my freshman year

Accomplishment #1:

_____

_____

Accomplishment #2:

_____

_____

Accomplishment #3:

_____

_____

Accomplishment #4:

_____

_____

Accomplishment #5:

_____

_____

EXERCISE 4.2: **Context for your Accomplishments**

DIRECTIONS: For each of your accomplishments, answer the following questions.

ACCOMPLISHMENT #1:

_____

_____

What was the specific situation, problem, or need that you had to deal with?

_____

_____

What actions did you take to manage the situation?

_____

_____

Identify the barriers that presented themselves.

_____

_____

What were the results that you achieved (be specific)?

_____

_____

What skills, abilities, or competencies did you learn?

_____

_____

ACCOMPLISHMENT #2:

_____

_____

What was the specific situation, problem, or need that you had to deal with?

_____

_____

What actions did you take to manage the situation?

_____

_____

Identify the barriers that presented themselves.

_____

_____

What were the results that you achieved (be specific)?

_____

_____

What skills, abilities, or competencies did you learn?

_____

_____

ACCOMPLISHMENT #3:

_____

_____

What was the specific situation, problem, or need that you had to deal with?

_____

_____

What actions did you take to manage the situation?

_____

_____

Identify the barriers that presented themselves.

_____

_____

What were the results that you achieved (be specific)?

_____

_____

What skills, abilities, or competencies did you learn?

_____

_____

ACCOMPLISHMENT #4:

_____

_____

What was the specific situation, problem, or need that you had to deal with?

_____

_____

What actions did you take to manage the situation?

_____

_____

Identify the barriers that presented themselves.

_____

_____

What were the results that you achieved (be specific)?

_____

_____

What skills, abilities, or competencies did you learn?

_____

_____

ACCOMPLISHMENT #5:

_____

_____

What was the specific situation, problem, or need that you had to deal with?

_____

_____

What actions did you take to manage the situation?

_____

_____

Identify the barriers that presented themselves.

_____

_____

What were the results that you achieved (be specific)?

_____

_____

What skills, abilities, or competencies did you learn?

_____

_____

EXERCISE 4.3: **Skills Analysis Grid**

DIRECTIONS:

1. Starting with your first accomplishment, place a check in Column #1 for every skill you feel that you used in that accomplishment.
2. Follow this process for each of your 5 accomplishments.
3. Working across, add up the number of checks for each row, and put the total (0-5) in the "total" column.

Note your top 5 skills based on the highest scores you find in the "total" column, and list them in the space provided at the bottom of this page.

SKILL	1.	2.	3.	4.	5.	TOTAL
Communication						
Listening						
Integrity						
Planning						
Using IT						
Financial Skills						
Creativity						
Research						
Selling						
Learning New Skills						
Coping in a Crisis						
Influencing						
Organizing						
Directing						
Coaching						
Leadership						
Decision-Making						

SKILL	1.	2.	3.	4.	5.	TOTAL
Presentation Skills						
Teamwork						
Time Management						
Dependable						
Goal Setting						
Conflict Management						
Judgment						
Critical Thinking						
Motivation						
Multi-tasking						
Problem-Solving						
Flexibility						
Loyal						
Confidence						
Determination						
Patience						
Empathy						

Top 5 Skills:

1. _____

2. _____

3. _____

4. _____

5. _____

MODULE 5

Researching the Job Market

Here's an example of labor market research: Did you know that there hasn't been a left-handed catcher in the major leagues since the year 1901, when Jiggs Donahue caught 19 games for the Milwaukee Brewers? Here's some more: Did you know the unemployment rate for people who recently earned undergraduate degrees in education is 5.7 percent, but 12.8 percent for recent architecture grads (Retrieved from Bureau of Labor Statistics: http://www.bls.gov)?

With this labor market data in hand, we can begin to draw a straightforward career conclusion: if you're left-handed, you may want to learn to play first base, as there has apparently been NO market for left- handed catchers in over 100 years. In the latter case, we can draw a different conclusion: if you are going to base career decisions at least in part on the availability of jobs in today's labor market, education looks like a smarter bet than architecture. Try this one: Do you have any idea how many jobs are out there for you to choose from?

There are two major sources of up-to-date job information. The Standard Occupational Classification system, used by the US Government, provides detailed descriptions on 840 current occupations. The federal Occupational Information Network (O*NET), provides information on more than 1,200 jobs. No wonder selecting an occupation is such a daunting task, there are too many options! With over 1,200 jobs to choose from, you will need to do some basic research in order to narrow down your choices to a manageable number.

Of course, researching the job market is similar in many ways to "game prep," and is nothing new to athletes. Have you ever watched game film on an opponent? Visited the site of an "away" match? Looked up the turnover stats on the opposing

> 66% of former athletes knew little to nothing about the job market as undergraduates

> *"Pay attention to the job trends and where the economy is heading while you're in school. Try to forecast where the needs will be and be absolutely sure you have a grasp of the particular job sector you are interested in pursuing. Research these jobs and set up a career plan. Understand salary and cost of living estimates for these jobs, and set up meetings to shadow older people in these roles."*
>
> —School Psychologist and Former Division II Men's Basketball Player

team's point guard? Checked out the earned run average of the opposing team's bullpen against left-handed hitting? Seen a scout sitting in the stands from an opposing team's staff? As an athlete, you have spent a lot of time trying to gain a better understanding, and thus a competitive edge, over an opponent before the opening whistle. This research is part of what it takes to be competitive in your sport. The world of work is no different. If you're going to be competitive in the race for the best jobs out there after graduation, you'll need to know how to use some basic research tools related to the job market.

The Career Game Plan will introduce you to some of the basic labor market research concepts. This research will help you make critically important decisions about the direction you'll take your academic (and other) pursuits both on campus, and into the world of work. This research is vital to understanding what kinds of specific jobs are supported in a competitive job market, what skills and credentials are required to land one of those jobs, and which actual employers might be seeking those skills.

Researching a Job Title

Most sports fans have only a limited understanding of just how grueling a full sports season can be. They come to a few games and read the scores and stories in the paper, but they don't really understand the day- in and day-out rigors of the full season. In the same way, without more solid information and data, deciding which profession is right for you can also be a difficult process. Taking the time now to understand how to thoroughly research various positions and industries will help you learn about various occupations' requirements, general responsibilities and, ultimately, their compatibility with your interests, strengths, and personality.

As a first step in exploring specific jobs and job families, it's important to review the *educational* requirements for the fields you are considering, especially as you select classes and potential majors. You should investigate the types of degrees and coursework to focus on now, while you are still fairly early in your college career. You'll also need to give some thought to exploring any related work experience that might give you a competitive edge after graduation, including part-time work on, or off, campus, volunteer work, or even internships. **Suggestion:** Learn the job titles, requirements, and other specifications in your professional areas of interest (consider utilizing your Strong Interest Inventory results), go to a couple of the larger job boards (Indeed, Monster, CareerBuilder), and look up 10-15 current job postings with those job titles. You can use these job postings to explore what job titles are in frequent use, and what the job market is requiring from successful candidates and hires. From here you can assess how your skills, experience, and qualifications stack up against the job description, the required qualifications, and the preferred qualifications. These job descriptions will help you think about future courses, internships, or contacts you should pursue to better qualify you for future employment in this career field. Although harder to ascertain through this kind of research, you'll also want to make an effort to match up the intangible requirements of the job with your own personality and values. For example, if you are an introvert, you may find a cold-calling sales job very difficult. Or, if you don't like the sight of blood, you may want to re-consider the medical side of healthcare.

Salary

Did you know that the average starting pay for minor league baseball players is between $1,100 and $2,150 a month, and is only paid during the season, which is sometimes only three months long? On the other hand, the average major league salary rose 5.4% in 2014, to a record $3.39 million a year (MLB Average Salary, 2013). Did you know that only one out of six baseball players drafted will make the majors, typically within five years (Gordon, 2014)? Makes a difference, doesn't it? Researching salaries can give you a realistic idea of the earning you can expect in various professions, and while money isn't everything, it is an important consideration in career planning. Knowing the average entry-level salary, as well as the range you can expect to earn over time can help you determine if this career path pays well enough to meet your lifestyle needs. And don't forget the overall monetary value that employee benefits, such as health insurance and tuition reimbursement, add to the overall compensation package. Did you know that the spouses and partners of commercial airline pilots and flight attendants can fly all over the world on a standby basis at greatly reduced rates? Similarly, did you know that if you are employed at a private university you often have your children's college tuition waived or your children can attend other colleges with reduced or no tuition cost? This could save you hundreds of thousands of dollars in college costs. Therefore, when analyzing salary, consider the entire package.

SUGGESTION:

1. Check out the following websites: www.payscale.org; www.salary.com; www.salaryexpert.com
2. Google: "salary surveys (insert job field/title here); *i.e.*, "salary survey occupational therapy"

Job Outlook

One thing that we know about the job market is that, like so many things, it will continue to change, often in dramatic ways, over the course of your working years. There are a number of jobs (as in the manufacturing sector, for example) that have shrunk in numbers over the last several years, while other jobs are coming into the job market that didn't even exist only a few years ago as health care needs grow for Baby Boomers and newer computer technologies emerge. As these trends continue, it will be increasingly important for you to get a solid idea of which direction the jobs or fields you're interested in are headed, and to recognize where there is potential for growth.

SUGGESTION: With your list of 3-5 specific occupational interests (see your Strong Interest Inventory results), visit the websites of the Occupational Outlook Handbook, CareerInfoNet, and the O*NET database to explore hiring trends and predictions for these job titles.

What Companies and Industries are Hiring?

To be a seismologist, it's going to helpful to live near a volcano. If you want to be an oceanographer or a deep sea fishing captain, it'll help to live on a coast. These are pretty obvious ones, but, in the long run, it's hard to get hired into a job if you don't know who can hire you. Identifying the top employers locally, regionally, or in global markets in your chosen field can make implementing later career choices and job search strategies a lot easier. On the other hand, if there is little or no demand for your skills or credentials in the markets or locations you want to live in, you'll need to alter course.

SUGGESTION: Use both general and locally-based job boards (Monster, CareerBuilder, etc.) to compile a preliminary list of potential employers that are posting openings for the kinds of jobs you've chosen to research. Then review these employer's websites, and explore them for potential job openings. The companies that you've uncovered might be the ones you'll want to seek out for informational meetings, internships, or even full-time employment in the semesters ahead, and/ or after graduation. No time like today to get started on this one!

Summary

In this section, and in the worksheet immediately to follow, we want to emphasize that in order to make smart, informed, and forward- looking decisions about the world of work, you'll need to master the basics of labor market research. Understand that the information you can uncover now, while you are on campus, can put you far ahead of your competition in both the broader lifelong process of career exploration, and in the more specific and nearer term challenge of finding a rewarding job after graduation. Specifically, we encourage to you to begin now to understand how best to:

- Uncover detailed information about the nature of specific jobs and job titles: educational requirements, experience needed to qualify for entry-level positions, and the less visible but equally important intangibles associated with those professions.
- Find detailed information about salary, compensation, and other rewards and benefits associated with specific professions.
- Research the predicted growth or decline rates associated with specific occupational families; and job titles.
- Learn to identify which specific companies and/or industries are most likely to have job openings, part-time work, or internships for you in your local or preferred geographical areas.

With this kind of information in hand, the game of finding meaningful and rewarding work after graduation just gets easier to master.

Career Spotlight

DAVID LAINO is a principal engineer at Endurance Wind Power. He played center for the basketball team at Rensselaer Polytechnic Institute until he graduated with a BS degree in Aeronautical Engineering.

EXERCISE

RATIONALE: In many ways, with so many choices available to recent college graduates, it is harder than ever to make good decisions about what majors to choose, what skills to develop, and what career paths to pursue. Yet, today there is a wealth of information available to support an informed career decision — although it's not always that easy to find. Once you know how to find it, though, you can conduct this kind of research over and over again — each time you choose to explore another career path. This exercise introduces you to the most common and best tools out there for this kind of career exploration.

EXERCISE 5.1: Labor Market Research

DIRECTIONS: For this exercise, you'll need to select one — and only one — career/occupation, so you can dig as deeply as possible into one job or job family. You can select any career or job title of interest to you for this exercise ("Commercial Pilot, High School Football Coach, Social Worker, US Senator...").

> *Hint: If you're not sure what to choose, you can go back to your Strong Interest Inventory results [see Module 3], and select an Occupation Title from the "Occupational Scales" section that you'd like to learn more about.*

As you go through the questions, you'll be introduced to several research sites and sources that are likely new to you. When you see these references *("Occupational Outlook Handbook"; "O*NET")*, just conduct a quick Google search to find out more on the research source. You might even want to bookmark these sites in your browser for future use!

Job title

_____

1. List any alternate or very similar job titles to the one that you selected.

    _____

    _____

2. Provide a brief occupational description for this job title from the _Occupational Outlook Handbook_.

    _____

    _____

    _____

3. Provide a brief occupational description for this job title from the _O*NET_.

    _____

    _____

    _____

4. What is the current number of jobs supported by the labor market in the occupation?

    # of jobs: _____

5. Is the demand for these types of jobs expected to increase or decrease in the next 5-10 years?

    Increasing or Decreasing (circle one) by _____%

6. What is the salary range or median wage or this occupation nationally?

    $_____ to $_____ per hour or annual

7. Based on your research, list **3** majors that would qualify a college graduate to pursue this vocational direction.

_____

_____

_____

8. Beyond a college degree, are there other certifications, licenses, or credentials that are required for this occupation?

_____

_____

_____

9. List **3** companies/employers/organizations within 100 miles of you right now that have job openings for this occupation.

_____

_____

_____

10. List up to **5** websites that you visited to gather this information: Other pertinent labor market information about your occupation.

_____

_____

_____

_____

_____

11. List any other research source that you found in the course of this search (personal interviews, etc.),

_____

_____

_____

Career Spotlight

JENNIFER KENNEDY is a Speech-Language Pathologist for Carolina's Healthcare System. She earned a Bachelors of Science and Masters degree in Communication Disorders from Appalachian State University. As an undergraduate, she was a member of the tennis team, and she continues to love the game today.

MODULE 6
The Myers-Briggs Type Indicator®

Many athletes tell us that, as youngsters, they were interested in playing whatever sport was in season. If you had the good fortune to attend a school or live in a neighborhood where leagues were well-organized, you may have rotated through any number of sports in your younger years, depending on the season. Perhaps, as you got older, you began to gravitate to a fewer number of sports, and — unless you're Bo Jackson or Deion Sanders– you finally settled into one primary sport or game of choice.

A number of factors certainly influence the choices that young athletes make: availability, cost of equipment, local sponsorship, and facilities, just to name a few. Yet, it is very likely that whether you were even aware of it or not, your personality also played a role in those choices. Do you remember feeling a preference, for example, for team sports versus individual sports? Contact sports versus non-contact sports?

This same kind of psychological process is present when we make career choices as well. You may recall from earlier in this text our emphasis on identifying a work setting that is consistent with your own unique personality, interests, and values as critical to long term career satisfaction. Earlier in Module 3, we used the Strong Interest Inventory to begin the process of identifying the types of careers that might align with your own interests and personality traits. In this section, we will add a new assessment to the mix, the *Myers-Briggs Type Indicator*® (MBTI®), in an effort to further build a sense of how a personality profile or assessment can point you toward a satisfying career path after graduation.

> 25% of former athletes indicated that they rarely to never considered looking for a job that aligned with their personality as undergraduates.

What is The MBTI?

The *Myers-Briggs Type Indicator®* (**MBTI®**) **assessment is said to be the most widely used personality inventory in the world, and is designed to help us better understand the way** that people tend to think, communicate, and interact with others. It is based on the psychological theories of Carl Jung, one of the early founders of modern psychoanalytic theory. His book, *Psychological Types*, was published in the 1930s, and reading it later caused the mother- daughter team of Isabel Briggs Myers and Katherine Cook Briggs to develop a paper-and- pencil (now computerized, of course) personality inventory, or test, during WWII. From those beginnings, the MBTI has grown significantly, and today many different kinds of MBTI profile reports are in use. The one you will be utilizing is designed specifically for college students and is intended to support students — like you — who are in the midst of identifying the most appropriate courses, majors, and potential career paths.

The Myers Briggs model provides insight into your personality based on four specific "preferences." We often use the analogy of handedness to help people understand what we mean by preferences. Consider this: When a baseball player first learns to hit, he usually finds that he has a "preference" for hitting from the right or the left side. Although we're not sure exactly why (was he born that way, or did he get better over time from one side of the plate via repetition and practice?), we see that mostly, after a while, ballplayers do in fact hit better from one side than the other. Yet, that same player uses his other, off-hand all the time for lots of things, including wearing a glove, and some players even learn to switch-hit. So, the MBTI theory is not an "all or nothing" theory; for example, to be right-handed is not to suggest that you never use your left. You just "prefer" the right hand for certain tasks.

For whatever reason, just as we do with handedness, we tend to make choices about how we organize our thinking and interact with others based on what feels more natural or is simply easier. In other words, while it is a function of your personality that you will demonstrate a preference for exhibiting some personality traits over others, it is also important to remember that you will also use "both hands" at one on time or another.

In MBTI terms, people have four preferences that are identified in the following categories:

- E or I (Extraversion or Introversion)
- S or N (Sensing or Intuition)
- T or F (Thinking or Feeling)
- J or P (Judgment or Perception)

The Four Preferences in more Detail

I. *Extraversion (E) v. Introversion (I)*. Where do you prefer to direct your energy?

- If you prefer to direct your energy to deal with people, things, situations, or "the outer world," then your preference is for **EXTRAVERSION**. This is denoted by the letter "E".
- If you prefer to direct your energy to deal with ideas, information, explanations, beliefs, or "the inner world," then your preference is for **INTROVERSION**. This is denoted by the letter "I."

II. *Sensing (S) v. Intuition (N)*. How do you prefer to process information?

- If you prefer to deal with facts, what you know, to have clarity, or to describe what you see, then your preference is for **SENSING**. This is denoted by the letter "S."
- If you prefer to deal with ideas, look into the unknown, to generate new possibilities, or to anticipate what isn't obvious, then your preference is for **INTUITION**. This is denoted by the letter "N." (Note that the letter I has already been used for Introversion.)

III. *Thinking (T) v. Feeling (F)*. How do you prefer to make decisions?

- If you prefer to decide on the basis of objective logic, using an analytic and detached approach, then your preference is for **THINKING**. This is denoted by the letter "T."
- If you prefer to decide using values and/or personal beliefs, on the basis of what you believe is important or what you or others care about, then your preference is for **FEELING**. This is denoted by the letter "F."

IV. *Judging (J) v. Perceiving (P)*. How do you prefer to organize your life?

- If you prefer your life to be planned, stable, and organized, then your preference is for **JUDGING** (not to be confused with 'Judgmental,' which is quite different). This is denoted by the letter "J."
- If you prefer to go with the flow, to maintain flexibility and respond to things as they arise, then your preference is for **PERCEPTION**. This is denoted by the letter "P."

When you combine the preferences for each of the four choices, you get your "Myers Briggs personality type," so having preferences (higher scores, really) for E and S and T and J, for example, gives a personality type of ESTJ. This generates a total of 16 possible Myers Briggs personality types. Below is a brief summary of 16 personality types.

SENSING TYPES		INTUITIVE TYPES		
ISTJ Quiet, serious, earn success by thoroughness and dependability. Practical, matter-of-fact, realistic, and responsible. Decide logically what should be done and work toward it steadily, regardless of distractions. Take pleasure in making everything orderly and organized – their work, their home, their life. Value traditions and loyalty.	**ISFJ** Quiet, friendly, responsible, and conscientious. Committed and steady in meeting their obligations. Thorough, painstaking, and accurate. Loyal, considerate, notice and remember specifics about people who are important to them, concerned with how others feel. Strive to create an orderly and harmonious environment at work and at home.	**INFJ** Seek meaning and connection in ideas, relationships, and material possessions. Want to understand what motivates people and are insightful about others. Conscientious and committed to their firm values. Develop a clear vision about how best to serve the common good. Organized and decisive in implementing their vision.	**INTJ** Have original minds and great drive for implementing their ideas and achieving their goals. Quickly see patterns in external events and develop long-range explanatory perspectives. When committed, organize a job and carry it through. Skeptical and independent, have high standards of competence and performance – for themselves and others.	INTROVERTS
ISTP Tolerant and flexible, quiet observers until a problem appears, then act quickly to find workable solutions. Analyze what makes things work and readily get through large amounts of data to isolate the core of practical problems. Interested in cause and effect, organize facts using logical principles, value efficiency.	**ISFP** Quiet, friendly, sensitive, and kind. Enjoy the present moment, what's going on around them. Like to have their own space and to work within their own time frame. Loyal and committed to their values and to people who are important to them. Dislike disagreements and conflicts, do not force their opinions or values on others.	**INFP** Idealistic, loyal to their values and to people who are important to them. Want an external life that is congruent with their values. Curious, quick to see possibilities, can be catalysts for implementing ideas. Seek to understand people and to help them fulfill their potential. Adaptable, flexible, and accepting unless a value is threatened.	**INTP** Seek to develop logical explanations for everything that interest them. Theoretical and abstract, interested more in ideas than in social interaction. Quiet, contained, flexible, and adaptable. Have unusual ability to focus in depth to solve problems in their area of interest. Skeptical, sometimes critical, always analytical.	
ESTP Flexible and tolerant, they take a pragmatic approach focused on immediate results. Theories and conceptual explanations bore them – they want to act energetically to solve the problem. Focus on the here-and-now, spontaneous, enjoy each moment that they can be active with others. Enjoy material comforts and style. Learn best through doing.	**ESFP** Outgoing, friendly, and accepting. Exuberant lovers of life, people, and material comforts. Enjoy working with others to make things happen. Bring common sense and a realistic approach to their work, and make work fun. Flexible and spontaneous, adapt readily to new people and environments. Learn best by trying a new skill with other people.	**ENFP** Warmly enthusiastic and imaginative. See life as full of possibilities. Make connections between events and information very quickly, and confidently proceed based on the patterns they see. Want a lot of affirmation from others, and readily give appreciation and support. Spontaneous and flexible, often rely on their ability to improvise and their verbal fluency.	**ENTP** Quick, ingenious, stimulating, alert, and outspoken. Resourceful in solving new and challenging problems. Adept at generating conceptual possibilities and then analyzing them strategically. Good at reading other people. Bored by routine, will seldom do the same things the same way, apt to turn to one new interest after another.	EXTRAVERTS
ESTJ Practical, realistic, matter-of-fact. Decisive, quickly move to implement decisions. Organize projects and people to get things done, focus on getting results in the most efficient way possible. Take care of routine details. Have a clear set of logical standards, systematically follow them and want others to also. Forceful in implementing their plans.	**ESFJ** Warmhearted, conscientious, and cooperative. Want harmony in their environment, work with determination to establish it. Like to work with others to complete tasks accurately and on time. Loyal, follow through even in small matters. Notice what others need in their day-today lives and try to provide it. Want to be appreciated for who they are and for what they contribute.	**ENFJ** Warm, empathetic, responsive, and responsible. Highly attuned to the emotions, needs, and motivations of others. Find potential in everyone, want to help others fulfill their potential. May act as catalysts for individual and group growth. Loyal, responsive to praise and criticism. Sociable, facilitate others in a group, and provide inspiring leadership.	**ENTJ** Frank, decisive, assume leadership readily. Quickly see illogical and inefficient procedures and policies, develop and implement comprehensive systems to solve organizational problems. Enjoy long-term planning and goal setting. Usually well informed, well read, enjoy expanding their knowledge and passing it on to others. Forceful in presenting their ideas.	

How MBTI Theory Affects Career Choice — An Exercise

"Most importantly I would try to play to my strengths and to find a career that makes me happy. I feel that I made choices based on some perceived sense of responsibility rather than on what I really enjoyed. I also allowed a lot of decisions to simply be made for me by not taking a more active role in deciding, starting with my major. I should have been a lot more aggressive in finding the right job for me."

—Electrical Engineer and Former Division I Volleyball Player

As part of a well- balanced assessment process, taking a close look at one's personality can be a genuine benefit as you struggle with the choices ahead: What classes should I take? What majors should I consider? What careers are interesting to me? The vast majority of college students find it difficult to define, describe, or even narrow down the kind of work they want to pursue. Having a greater appreciation for your personality preferences can help you brainstorm, research, evaluate, and even recognize the kind of work that can bring you the maximum amount of career satisfaction.

Let's take a look at some very practical applications from the MBTI profile of Larry Lacrosse, for example. Larry thinks he might want to go into the education field. His mother was a teacher, and he has been doing some tutoring in the computer lab as a part of his work-study program. He took the MBTI last week, and his profile was ENFP. As a part of his career exploration, he has been asked by his instructors to develop a short list of possible job titles or roles within the field of education that he would like to explore further. Using only the information presented in the chart above, and taking into account Larry's MBTI type as a guide, how would you answer these questions for Larry?

1. *One area that Larry seems to be drawn to is the area of special education, and specifically working with kids in the early elementary school grade with mental difficulties. Are there any aspects of Larry's personality that might make this a good — or a bad — choice for him?*

_____

_____

_____

_____

2. *He is also looking at becoming a high school counselor, where he might primarily work with students in a one-on-one setting, helping them with such issues as college scholarship and financial aid applications, social, or emotional difficulties fitting in in their classrooms, or helping them resolve disputes with other students. What aspects of his MBTI results might he consider as he looks at this area?*

_____

_____

_____

_____

3. *Larry thinks he would like to be a teacher at the high school level, but will have to earn a degree in the area that he would teach in order to be certified at the high school level. What majors might be good — or bad — ones for him to consider?*

_____

_____

_____

_____

Summary

The Myers Briggs Type Indicator, or MBTI, is a widely used personality assessment, and has been used to help people better understand the way they think, communicate, and interact with others. It has been used specifically as an aid to help people who are wrestling with career choice issues, as we know that people are more attracted to, and are typically happier, when their careers allow them to make use of natural personality preferences.

As you review your own MBTI profile, you may find that your results can shed some additional light on a number of the choices that you will face in the semesters (and years!) ahead. These include:

- The MBTI can help you identify (and maybe also rule out) potential classes, majors, and specific career paths according to your personality preferences. You can use these results while you're still on campus.

- It can increase your awareness of your own learning style, so you can be more successful in the way that you study, absorb information, and manage various classroom assignments and requirements.

- Having a better grasp of your personality type can also help you more comfortably manage the nuts and bolts of your actual job search after graduation, from resume writing and design to interview preparation, to weighing the pros and cons of an actual job offer. The better you know yourself, your traits, and your motivators, the easier you'll find it to communicate these important issues to others when the search is on.

Career Spotlight

MIKE TARVER is currently a Business Initiatives Consultant at Wells Fargo. He graduated from Davidson College with a Bachelor's of Arts degree in Economics, and played wide receiver for the football team.

ACTIVITIES

RATIONALE: Your results on the Myers Briggs Type Indicator are intended to help you better understand the way both you and others tend to think, communicate, and interact with one another. The test is extensively used to provide insight into vocational choice and direction. The worksheet below is simply designed to capture the key points that you will want to retain and think about from this report. As you did with Strong Interest Inventory in Module 3, you'll use this worksheet to integrate these results, and your reaction to them, into the additional assessment tools you'll be exposed to throughout the course of this program.

EXERCISE 6.1: Your Type

DIRECTIONS: After completing the MBTI, circle your type (based on your results)

E – Extraversion People who prefer Extraversion tend to focus on the outer world of people and things.	**I – Introversion** People who prefer Introversion tend to focus on the inner world of ideas and impressions.
S – Sensing People who prefer Sensing tend to focus on the present and on concrete information gained from their senses.	**N – Intuition** People who prefer Intuition tend to focus on the future, with a view toward patterns and possibilities.
T – Thinking People who prefer Thinking tend to base their decisions primarily on logic and on objective analysis of cause and effect.	**F – Feeling** People who prefer Feeling tend to base their decisions primarily on values and on subjective evaluation of person-centered concerns.
J – Judging People who prefer Judging tend to like a planned and organized approach to life and prefer to have things settled.	**P – Perceiving** People who prefer Perceiving tend to like a flexible and spontaneous approach to life and prefer to keep their options open.

EXERCISE 6.2: **Key Traits**

DIRECTIONS: After completing the MBTI, find your type below (from the 16 possible combinations) and underline or highlight the key traits that represent you most accurately.

ISTJ

Quiet, serious, earn success by thoroughness and dependability. Practical, matter-of-fact, realistic, and responsible. Decide logically what should be done and work toward it steadily, regardless of distractions. Take pleasure in making everything orderly and organized - their work, their home, their life. Value traditions and loyalty.

ISFJ

Quiet, friendly, responsible, and conscientious. Committed and steady in meeting their obligations. Thorough, painstaking, and accurate. Loyal, considerate, notice and remember specifics about people who are important to them, concerned with how others feel. Strive to create an orderly and harmonious environment at work and at home.

INFJ

Seek meaning and connection in ideas, relationships, and material possessions. Want to understand what motivates people and are insightful about others. Conscientious and committed to their firm values. Develop a clear vision about how best to serve the common good. Organized and decisive in implementing their vision.

INTJ

Have original minds and great drive for implementing their ideas and achieving their goals. Quickly see patterns in external events and develop long-range explanatory perspectives. When committed, organize a job and carry it through. Skeptical and independent, have high standards of competence and performance - for themselves and others.

ISTP

Tolerant and flexible, quiet observers until a problem appears, then act quickly to find workable solutions. Analyze what makes things work and readily get through large amounts of data to isolate the core of practical problems. Interested in cause and effect, organize facts using logical principles, value efficiency.

ISFP

Quiet, friendly, sensitive, and kind. Enjoy the present moment, what's going on around them. Like to have their own space and to work within their own time frame. Loyal and committed to their values and to people who are important to them. Dislike disagreements and conflicts, do not force their opinions or values on others.

INFP

Idealistic, loyal to their values and to people who are important to them. Want an external life that is congruent with their values. Curious, quick to see possibilities, can be catalysts for implementing ideas. 81
Seek to understand people and to help them fulfill their potential. Adaptable, flexible, and accepting unless a value is threatened.

INTP

Seek to develop logical explanations for everything that interests them. Theoretical and abstract, interested more in ideas than in social interaction. Quiet, contained, flexible, and adaptable. Have unusual ability to focus in depth to solve problems in their area of interest. Skeptical, sometimes critical, always analytical.

ESTP

Flexible and tolerant, they take a pragmatic approach focused on immediate results. Theories and conceptual explanations bore them - they want to act energetically to solve the problem. Focus on the here-and-now, spontaneous, enjoy each moment that they can be active withothers. Enjoy material comforts and style. Learn best through doing.

ESFP

Outgoing, friendly, and accepting. Exuberant lovers of life, people, and material comforts. Enjoy working with others to make things happen. Bring common sense and a realistic approach to their work, and make work fun. Flexible and spontaneous, adapt readily to new people and environments. Learn best by trying a new skill with other people.

ENFP

Warmly enthusiastic and imaginative. See life as full of possibilities. Make connections between events and information very quickly, and confidently proceed based on the patterns they see. Want a lot of affirmation from others, and readily give appreciation and support. Spontaneous and flexible, often rely on their ability to improvise and their verbal fluency.

ENTP

Quick, ingenious, stimulating, alert, and outspoken. Resourceful in solving new and challenging problems. Adept at generating conceptual possibilities and then analyzing them strategically. Good at reading other people. Bored by routine, will seldom do the same thing the same way, apt to turn to one new interest after another.

ESTJ

Practical, realistic, matter-of-fact. Decisive, quickly move to implement decisions. Organize projects and people to get things done, focus on getting results in the most efficient way possible. Take care of routine details. Have a clear set of logical standards, systematically follow them and want others to also. Forceful in implementing their plans.

ESFJ

Warmhearted, conscientious, and cooperative. Want harmony in their environment, work with determination to establish it. Like to work with others to complete tasks accurately and on time. Loyal, follow through even in small matters. Notice what others need in their day-by-day lives and try to provide it. Want to be appreciated for who they are and for what they contribute.82

ENFJ

Warm, empathetic, responsive, and responsible. Highly attuned to the emotions, needs, and motivations of others. Find potential in everyone, want to help others fulfill their potential. May act as catalysts for individual and group growth. Loyal, responsive to praise and criticism. Sociable, facilitate others in a group, and provide inspiring leadership.

ENTJ

Frank, decisive, assume leadership readily. Quickly see illogical and inefficient procedures and policies, develop and implement comprehensive systems to solve organizational problems. Enjoy long-term planning and goal setting. Usually well informed, well read, enjoy expanding their knowledge and passing it on to others. Forceful in presenting their ideas. Excerpted from Introduction to Type® by Isabel Briggs Myers published by CPP. Inc. Used with permission.

EXERCISE 6.3: MBTI Career Implications

DIRECTIONS: Based on your MBTI results, identify 5 traits that might have an impact on your career exploration.

Key Traits

1. _____

2. _____

3. _____

4. _____

5. _____

Career Spotlight

ERIC KING is currently a Director of Sales Operations at AT&T Communications. He graduated from Jacksonville State University with Bachelor of Science degrees in both Marketing and Finance, where he played strong safety for the 1992 National Champion JSU Gamecocks. He later earned his MBA in Strategic Management from DePaul University in Chicago.

MODULE 7

Resume Basics

Collage coaches recruit talent based in part on watching the athlete in actual competition. Yet, recruiters and coaches also typically compile a summary of an athlete's personal and team statistics, playing experience, education, grade point average, and accomplishments both on and off the field, long before scholarship offers are extended. In the working world, while there's not a lot of game film involved when employers recruit their employees, the rest of the early talent evaluation process is almost identical to the sports world. In sports, your background might be summed up in a written evaluation or file, for example. In the world of work, consider your resume in the same way.

What is a Resume?

A resume is a written compilation of your education, work experience, credentials, and accomplishments. It is the first and foremost tool used to apply for professional level jobs. It is typically a brief document (maximum two pages), and, in your case as a college student or recent college graduate, it will likely be approximately one page in length. It will include a brief summary that records factors from your background that are relevant to your qualifications for a particular job. A resume is generally attached to a job application (typically online). The purpose of your resume is to introduce yourself to the potential employer quickly and in a format that's easy to digest — and to get you an interview.

Because it is intended to be a *brief* summary of your experience, it should be written as concisely as possible. The style and "voice" of resumes are different than that of letters and papers, and often use sentence fragments and bulleted lists rather than long sentences and paragraphs, so that the reader can glance over the document quickly. The typical resume reader spend 10 seconds on a resume before making a "go or no-go" decision to contact you for an interview.

Yet, a resume is more than merely a list of experiences. It is also a selling tool that outlines your skills and experiences so employers can quickly assess how you can contribute to their

> 26% of former athletes indicated that as undergraduates they knew little to nothing about what information should be included on a resume.

needs. The most effective resumes are focused on a specific job title and address your targeted employer's particular requirements for that position. Therefore, the more you know about the duties and skills necessary for a job, the more effectively you can write the resume to get you that first interview.

A good resume includes your most relevant accomplishments, skills, and experience for the specific job to which you're applying. Therefore, the more you know now about the work you may want pursue after graduation, the more you can tailor your resume to fit the job market. In summary, a resume is a self-marketing tool. Its purpose is to effectively communicate your assets in writing to an employer. In order to craft the best resume possible, you'll need to be aware of your own skills and qualifications, what employers want, and where there is a match between the two. If you can present that information in a clear, easy-to-follow format, you'll get those interviews!

In this section, we will introduce you to the general content of a solid resume, including suggestions for what kinds of information you should begin to gather and record right away. At the end of this section, we will provide you with a template, and we'll encourage you to begin to fill in the sections with the information suggested. This will help you accomplish the following:

1. It will give you the chance to start gathering and storing information relevant to your resume as you go through this program. A good resume is a living and breathing document, and you'll find that savvy job seekers are constantly upgrading, updating, or reconsidering the content of their resume.

2. For now, don't be overly worried about what content goes where, or in what order. If you know that the information is relevant, and that it's is likely to fit somewhere, just go ahead and put it down. In subsequent sessions we'll begin to translate this important document from a list of facts and data to a piece of work that actually tells a story — the story of your background, plans, progress, and career trajectory.

3. Do you have sections of this resume template that you can't fill in? Those sections will be just as important (if not more important) as the sections you can complete. Identifying the gaps on your resume will give you a road map for the kinds of experiences, educational offerings, or campus involvement that you will need to complete in order to add to your career portfolio. It is important to understand your gaps now, while you still have time on campus to do something about it.

What's In A Resume?

A HEADING: Assuming resume readers like what they read in the body of your resume, the next step will be for them to contact you to discuss next steps in the screening process. If this is not an easy task for them, you're likely to get passed over for the next (maybe by an even less qualified) candidate. Be sure to include your full name, along with such contact information as:

- **EMAIL ADDRESS:** Your email address should be as close to your full name (for example first-name.lastname@gmail.com) as possible. In all correspondence and communications, you'll want to be recognizable by the resume reader at a glance. No cute nicknames allowed in the job search! Consider formatting your resume in such a way that your email address is hyperlinked, so that if it is being read in electronic form, the reader can simply click on your address to contact you easily.

- **PHONE NUMBER:** For resume purposes, the phone number listed should be your primary number, one that you that you have full access to, and one that others typically DON'T have access to. The most well-meaning people in your life may answer the phone in a non-professional way, or forget to pass on important professional messages in a timely way. Don't let that happen to you; keep control of your telecommunications.

- **MAILING ADDRESS:** Some experts are recommending that you leave off your mailing address these days to protect your privacy, and you too can do that if you choose. Yet, if you choose this option, you should still include your city/state in your heading. In today's competitive workplace, sometimes local job candidates are given a slight preference in the job search process, as the cost of relocating employees is not always a part of the hiring budget for some positions.

A SUMMARY OR AN OBJECTIVE: You may choose to start off your resume with an *Objective*, which is a forward-looking statement ("Seeking an opportunity to work in the field of healthcare…"), or a *Summary*, which looks back at your accumulated experiences ("Over three years of experience working in the health care field, including…"). In either case, this section is of critical importance, as it may be the only part of the resume that prospective employers read before deciding to contact you to move forward in the screening process. Because of this, we advise you to actually compose your resume first, then re-read the whole thing, in order to pick out those aspects of the whole story that are best suited to the job you are pursuing. You'll find it a lot easier to compose the Summary/Objective statement if you write this section last.

With the wonders of word processing, this section of your resume can be tailored individually to almost every job you apply for. Still, you will want to identify the core credentials, experiences, and qualifications you will bring to your post- graduation job. By the way, this section can have a lot of other headings/labels as well: Career Summary, Summary of Qualifications, Career Highlights, Professional Profile, or Career Aspirations, to name a few.

EDUCATION/ACADEMIC ACCOMPLISHMENTS: The best placement of this section is open to debate. We typically recommend it go immediately after your Summary, closer to the top of the resume, as this information represents the most recent and important accomplishments in your toolkit as a relatively young, entry- level worker. However, we will often recommend that you should drop this section closer to the bottom, particularly if your actual work experience is your best competitive advantage over other entry level workers. For now, don't worry too much about WHERE it goes. Just be sure to begin to gather and record the necessary and relevant information; you'll find the right spot for it later. Along with your degree and major, you may choose to include:

- GPA
- Academic honors
- Scholarship awards
- Senior project, honors paper, poster presentation
- Examples of team projects (and your specific role on that team)
- Specific relevant coursework
- Any relevant continuing educational coursework or training that you received outside the formal classroom (Red Cross Safety Certification, CPR, etc.)

"I think it is critical for student-athletes to start building their resume in their freshman and sophomore years. It is critical for students to begin preparing early for eventual entry into the job market. Your academic transcript and college resume is built over 3-4 years. You cannot cram everything in the last couple of semesters and expect to be competitive against your competition."

—Pharmacist and Former Division I Football Player

PROFESSIONAL EXPERIENCE: The professional experience section allows you to present those actual jobs you've held, whether full-time, part- time, summer jobs, internships, co-ops, or others. This is your opportunity to demonstrate that you have experience in the actual "real world" of the workplace and to showcase your transferable skills to the job you are applying for.

First, you should list the employer, the dates of employment, and the job title(s) you held. Next, you should describe what the job entailed — what you actually did and what tasks you were responsible for. Additionally, you can list one or two specific accomplishments that you are proud of from that work experience. (Of course, if any of them can be taken directly from the work that you did in listing your accomplishments in Module 4 of this program, all the better.) An accomplishment statement should include what you did to improve the circumstances, and the results of your efforts, such as: *"Coordinated a United Way fund drive for all employees that contributed over $3,000 to the local homeless shelter in 2014."*

EXTRACURRICULAR ON-CAMPUS ACTIVITIES: Employers are looking for candidates with transferable skills and experience. In some cases, your job titles, education, and credentials may not provide employers with enough evidence of your skill set. In this case, listing your extracurricular activities on a resume can round out your qualifications and distinguish you among the other applicants, giving you an edge in the hiring process. Of course, for you, this is the spot on the resume that should feature your athletic experience and accomplishments. Both team and individual accomplishments should be displayed prominently in this section. Beyond this, you may also want to consider including any of the following:

- Leadership experience (off the playing field) in clubs, organizations, or service groups
- Volunteer and service activities
- Campus jobs, resident assistant position
- Foreign languages

- Peer mentoring/tutoring activities
- Performing arts activities (music, drama, theater)
- Study abroad

OPTIONAL HEADINGS/SECTIONS: There are a number of potential optional sections that you may choose to include in your first resume draft, such as:

- Computer skills
- Honors and awards
- Hobbies and interests
- Foreign travel
- Community service
- Membership in professional groups related to your career field

Sample Resume:

DANIELLE CHRISTINE

506-295-5555   danielle.christine@gmail.com

MARKETING / COMMUNICATIONS / PUBLIC RELATIONS

Summer 2014 graduate in Corporate Communications with Fortune 500 internship experience, a 4-year record of philanthropic and leadership experience in a university/sorority setting, and previous work experience in Food Service/Hospitality settings. Selected participant, California Governor's School for the Arts. Excellent work ethic, very extroverted personality, and stellar professional and personal references.

SELECTED PROFESSIONAL EXPERIENCES

BROWN-FIRSTMAN — San Jose, CA   **Summer 2013 & 2014**
Among the top 10 global beverage companies, B-F sells its brands, including Gatorade, in 135 countries.

Public Relations Intern (Summer 2014)
Under the direct supervision of the VP Director of Public Relations, gained hands-on experience in social/interactive media, product launches, press relations, crisis management, press kits / releases, and marketing presentations, with an emphasis on building brand loyalty among Millennials (age 21 — 30). Projects included:

THE CAREER GAME PLAN

- **Kentucky Derby:** Participated in all marketing/public relations activities on site at Churchill Downs, including media spots and media relations on Derby and Oaks Day. Created Excel spreadsheet for senior management to report all media hits on television, radio, newspaper, magazine, and websites around the U.S. for all brands participating in KY Derby events. Also supported $1K Mint Hill Cup charity event.
- **Marketing to Millennials**: Conducted initial research and interviewed 21- 25 year old consumers to create a list of over 100 websites by category to target Millennial buyers. Worked as a team member that built and presented "Building Brand Loyalty among Millennials" to 25 B-F full-time employees.

Brand Marketing Intern (Summer 2013)
Reported directly to the VP Brand Director, in support of new product launch initiatives. Work assignments provided hands-on exposure to press kits, teaser kits, video editing, design, pitching media, writing copy and the creation of additional materials to support new brand roll-outs. Significant work in social media.

- **Consumer Planning Video:** Cut and edited 12-15 hours of interview footage from retailers and bartenders from around the U.S. and grouped responses in relevant themes. Met directly with professional editing agency to finalize video to be presented to Brown-Firstman employees at Strategy & Ideation conference in Las Vegas, Nevada.
- **Brand History Brochure:** Worked directly with Marketing Specialist, Global Marketing Director, and Designer to implement new design, creative, and text for history brochure that was distributed to media, employees, consumers, and retailers all over the world.

Salty Dog Café — Hilton Head Island SC — Food Server   2012

Lakeside Swim Club — Louisville, KY — Life Guard (CPR / First Aid-certified)   2009-2011

EDUCATION

B.S., Corporate Communications — University of Kentucky — Lexington, KY   Summer 2014
- Delta Chi House Manager. Convened membership meetings, served as sorority liaison to the University Housing department, worked with vendors and suppliers to implement housing improvement expenditures.
- Organizer and Fundraiser: "The Main Event". Participated in the solicitation of 8-10 corporate sponsorships and the sales of 5,000 individual tickets to this event, raising $40K for the Huntsman Cancer Institute.
- Contributor and volunteer for DANCE BLUE, the largest student-run philanthropic organization in Kentucky. Hosted fundraising events, solicited direct donations, and participated in the 24-hour marathon. DANCE BLUE contributed nearly $835K to the University of Kentucky's Pediatric Oncology Clinic in 2012.

Summary

This module is designed to ensure that you are fully aware of the kinds of information that you should start gathering now in order to create the best and most competitive resume you can. Using the template/worksheet below will help you gather and record the information currently available to you, and will also highlight the things you'll need to pay attention to in order to fill any blanks before graduation.

Remember, a resume is a written compilation of your education, work experience, credentials, and accomplishments, and the first and foremost tool used to apply for professional level jobs. It is also a selling tool that tells a potential employer how you can contribute to their needs. Finally, the best resumes not only tell YOUR story, but they also reflect the research you've done to assure that your story matches up well with what employers in your chosen vocational areas want and need in their employees.

Career Spotlight

DAUNTAE FINGER is currently a Team Sales Representative at Eastbay. He graduated from the University of North Carolina at Chapel Hill with a degree in Communications. While at UNC, he was a tight end on the football team.

EXERCISE

RATIONALE: When drafting a resume for the first time, starting with a blank piece of paper or computer screen can be truly overwhelming. On the other hand, if you start the process now, and begin to gather and record some of the key information you'll need, before all that information starts to fade from memory, the resume writing and design process will be significantly easier a little further down the road. This is one of those exercises that will pay big dividends later if you take it seriously now. Of course, you should return to this exercise once a semester or at least at the end of each academic year throughout your college career, adding relevant information as it occurs.

EXERCISE 7.1: Compiling Resume Data

DIRECTIONS: For each of the categories below, list all of the relevant data that could be included on a resume.

1. Past employers and internships — job titles, job duties, accomplishments, dates, locations, supervisors

   _____

   _____

   _____

   _____

   _____

   _____

   _____

   _____

_____

_____

_____

_____

2. Academic awards, scholarships, accomplishments

_____

_____

_____

_____

3. Volunteer/community activity

_____

_____

_____

_____

4. Extracurricular on-campus activities

_____

_____

_____

_____

_____

5. Computer skills

    _____

    _____

    _____

    _____

    _____

    _____

6. Athletic accomplishments

    _____

    _____

    _____

    _____

    _____

    _____

7. Leadership experience

    _____

    _____

    _____

    _____

    _____

    _____

8. Foreign languages and proficiency

_____

_____

_____

_____

_____

_____

9. Hobbies and interests

_____

_____

_____

_____

_____

_____

10. Professional organizations

_____

_____

_____

_____

_____

_____

MODULE 8
Identifying Your Career Values

The National Association of Intercollegiate Athletics (NAIA) created a program a few years ago called "Champions of Character." Its mission is to promote what the NAIA considers to be a set of five core values, so that "students, coaches, and parents know, do, and value the right thing on and off the field." In other words, the NAIA has identified what it believes to be the core values that are central to the college student- athlete experience (Five Core Values, 2015). Here are those values, along with a brief definition of each of them:

> **INTEGRITY:** Know and do what is right.
> **RESPECT:** Treat others the way you want to be treated.
> **RESPONSIBILITY:** Embrace opportunities to contribute.
> **SPORTSMANSHIP:** Bring your best to all competition.
> **SERVANT LEADERSHIP:** Serve the common good.

The NCAA, like the NAIA, has a set of core values that it expects to guide its athletes and member institutions (NCAA Core Values, 2015). The NCAA's core values are:

> **The collegiate model of athletics** in which students participate as an avocation, balancing their academic, social, and athletics experiences.
>
> **The highest levels of integrity and sportsmanship**.

The pursuit of excellence in both academics and athletics.

The supporting role that intercollegiate athletics plays in the higher education mission and in enhancing the sense of community and strengthening the identity of member institutions.

An inclusive culture that fosters equitable participation for student-athletes and career opportunities for coaches and administrators from diverse backgrounds.

Respect for institutional autonomy and philosophical differences.

Presidential leadership of intercollegiate athletics at the campus, conference, and national levels.

You may or may not agree that these values are the ones that should apply to all college athletes, or that these are the five that you would come up with if you were asked. Yet, it is an interesting idea that there is a set of values that apply to the world of college athletics.

It is equally challenging to imagine that, in the world of work, a single set of guiding values could exist that would help us identify potential employers with the "right" values, or a work settings that aligns with our own belief system. In fact, your experiences with the two assessments that you've taken in previous sections suggest that there are Six General Occupational Themes (GOT) in the Strong Interest Inventory and 16 different personality "types" as defined by the Myers Briggs Type Indicator. But what about our work values? How many are there? 16? 6? An unlimited number? And how do these values apply to the world of work?

What are Values?

Values are considered to be the most important guiding principles to help you set priorities, in your career and in your life. Values are typically highly personal and assist in defining what is meaningful to you. Your values, then, serve as a kind of moral compass as you set goals and make decisions.

Your values are the things or ideals that you have — or will adopt — as guiding principles. They will have a significant impact on you as you decide what is important and satisfying to you in life

25% of former athletes stated that they rarely to never considered looking for a job that aligned with their values as an undergraduate.

and at work. These values, whether you have identified, defined, or recorded them or not, will play a role in practically all the plans and decisions you make. They can come from a checklist — like the one at the end of this module — or they can be highly personal ones that you have identified or decided on by yourself. As these values become clearer to you, they will give you a way to define for yourself what matters the most in your life.

You will very likely use these values as measuring sticks, and if you make choices that are consistent with these values, you'll probably feel that you made the right decision, chose the right major, or are pursuing the right career path. On the other hand, if you find yourself feeling uncomfortable with certain choices or decisions you've made, a conflict between your values and the things you are actually doing (your behaviors) probably exists.

Regardless of the arena — athletics or managing your career — making a conscious effort to identify your values is of critical importance. Your values could (and possibly should) be the most important guiding principle that helps you set your priorities. In a career context, it is critical to reflect on the values that are most essential to you whenever you make important career decisions.

Workplace Values

Identifying and finding work that will fit with your personal and professional values is no easy task. For example, perhaps you have already begun to ask yourself these kinds of questions:

- What do I hope to get out of my first "real" job after college? Money? A learning experience? A resume builder? Prestige? Public recognition? Something that will make my parents proud? Contribution to community?
- What career path (of those I have explored or thought about so far) will make me feel the best about myself?
- How will my first job affect my relationships with my closest friends and family?
- What do I hope that my next employer contributes to society?
- What will others think of me when I tell them where I work or what I do?
- How has the very competitive environment I've been a part of while here at school affected the way I see the world of work?

Understanding how your values are aligned with your major, your job, or your next employer can play a large role in pursuing career paths and attaining a higher level of career-related satisfaction and motivation. Perhaps the simplest of many different ways to look at values in groups is to think in terms of **INTRINSIC VALUES and EXTRINSIC VALUES**:

"I would certainly try to figure out what my work related values were and how they could translate into a career direction. Because you will never truly be fulfilled in a job that does not align with your values."

—Speech Therapist and Former Division I Women's Gymnast

INTRINSIC values are those that really seem to reside inside of you, and make up who you are as a person, wherever you might be or whatever the circumstances. Some people have a value that could be articulated best as "family comes first." For example, a parent with this essential value might place a higher priority on raising children than on achievements in the workplace. If this is the case, then you can predict that some career decisions will be secondary to that value or belief. They may choose to leave work every day at 5pm versus working longer hours — even if working more hours is expected to earn a promotion. Individuals with this value may choose to enter a profession where they could work in a school, for example, so they could be home when the kids got out of school. When we think of intrinsic values, we are asking a question of ourselves that is very individualized, like "What would motivate me to truly love my work day after day?" and "What trade-offs am I willing to make to live out these values while in the world of work?"

EXTRINSIC values, on the other hand, are those that exist out in the world that are external to us; they are often reactions to the things that go on in the environment around us. In the world of work, for example, the easiest extrinsic value to identify is the idea of how important earning a large salary is to your career satisfaction. While it is of course possible to make a reasonable salary in a number of different career paths, we also know that some college majors and career paths will directly offer higher salaries. For example, engineering and technical majors and career paths tend to offer higher starting salaries than liberal arts majors. Another example of an extrinsic value might be related to the work environment. Do you want to work indoors or outside? Is a nice office with air conditioning and a coffee pot important to you? Routine or variety? Would you prefer the opportunity to work from home or the camaraderie and fellowship of a more traditional work setting, such as a hospital or a school? Do you feel strongly about a being a member of a diverse work force? Extrinsic values are important to think about early and often because we all have needs and things that we expect from an employer. Understanding your values will allow you to effectively evaluate your fit within an organization.

Summary

We have defined values as our guiding principles and the things to which we commit. Some of these will stay constant throughout our lives, while others will change as the circumstances in one's life change. These are the things that motivate us to succeed and that contribute in significant ways to ongoing career satisfaction.

Take a look back at the career assessment process that you have undergone since you began this program. You have now had a chance to take a closer look at your personality through the MBTI, career interests through the SII, and your work-related intrinsic and extrinsic values. You should refer to these assessment results often as your career begins to unfold. Many people who have experienced great professional success have found this kind of insight to have a profound effect on their ability to find and perform work that is meaningful and satisfying.

Career Spotlight

SHARON GLOVER is currently the Training Manager for Ecolab. She graduated from Boise State University with a Bachelor's of Arts degree in English, where she was a sprinter for the track and field team. Sharon also earned a Masters of Human Relations from the University of Oklahoma.

EXERCISE

RATIONALE: As you continue to add data to your career assessment portfolio, you'll begin to notice some trends and recurring results. Once again, to get the most out of an assessment process, you should continuously examine and evaluate those results, comparing previous reports and conclusions with others, looking for — and thinking about — both consistencies and inconsistencies. The Career Values Exercise is the last piece of the assessment puzzle in this program, so you should use this worksheet to record these results, and your reaction to them, into the larger portfolio of assessment results.

EXERCISE 8.1: Your Personal and Workplace Values

DIRECTIONS: From the list of values, identify your top 5 personal and workplace values and place them in the chart. If there are some terms that come to mind that are not listed, please add them to the list in the blank spaces. There may be one or more values that appear on both lists.

Variety	Achievement	Creativity
Autonomy	Challenge	Sense of Community
Competition	Cultural Diversity	Excitement
Recognition/Fame	Independence	Friendships
Fun	Helping Others	Influence
Impact Society	Knowledge	Learning
Personal Development	Legacy	Balance
Power	Loyalty	Stability/Security
Risk	Teamwork	Affiliation
Efficiency	Excellence	Relationships
Reputation	Responsibility/Accountability	Self-Respect
Time Freedom/Flexibility	Wealth	Leadership
Intensity	Aesthetics	_____
_____	_____	_____

Personal Values: Workplace Values

1. _____   _____

2. _____   _____

3. _____   _____

4. _____   _____

5. _____   _____

VALUES: Definition of Terms

VARIETY: enjoying different types of activities and having an appreciation for new and different things; flexibility

ACHIEVEMENT: feeling a sense of mastery or sense of accomplishment

AUTONOMY: ability to work alone or independently, with little oversight or management; a need for freedom in work

CREATIVITY: ability and appreciation for tasks requiring imagination or innovation; something allowing for the development of new ideas; artistic expression

CHALLENGE: the desire to push yourself and stretch in order to learn and grow; enjoying the sense of accomplishment received from achieving difficult tasks

SENSE OF COMMUNITY: the need to feel connected and integrated into a larger group of people

COMPETITION: striving to be the best within a group; enjoying being put against others

CULTURAL DIVERSITY: being surrounded by people from various backgrounds, cultures, experiences, and beliefs 104

EXCITEMENT: drama, fast-pace, sense of adventure, high stimulation

RECOGNITION/FAME: receiving public accolades and credit for efforts and achievements; having others admire and look up to you

INDEPENDENCE: flexibility and freedom; being able to have some control over the direction and details of what you do

FRIENDSHIPS: developing good relationships with others through working together that may be able to expand to multiple areas

FUN: freedom to be playful and enjoy yourself; entertaining

HELPING OTHERS: assisting or serving people directly, either individuals or groups

INFLUENCE: having the ability or opportunity to change or shape decisions, people, or organizations

IMPACT SOCIETY: contributing to the growth and development of the larger community or world

KNOWLEDGE: ability to learn, understand, and develop, either by experience or observation

LEARNING: continual acquisition of knowledge

PERSONAL DEVELOPMENT: opportunity to be self-reflective and integrate experiences to allow for growth

LEGACY: being able to leave a mark for others to remember you by

BALANCE: being able to provide the appropriate amount of energy to multiple areas

POWER: the ability to control or influence the behaviors of others or being able to impact the outcome of important events

LOYALTY: being able to commit or provide unwavering support to an institution or environment; feeling a sense of institutional or environmental support 105

STABILITY/SECURITY: consistency and predictability; an environment or situation that is likely to remain the same

RISK: Sense of challenge or danger; the presence of potential for high success or failure

TEAMWORK: opportunities for collaboration or the need to work with others to accomplish a goal

EFFICIENCY: maximizing outcome with limited wasted effort or energy

EXCELLENCE: consistently creating high quality outcomes

RELATIONSHIPS: placing high value on interactions between individuals; wanting to be deeply connected to other people

REPUTATION: placing high value on how others view you and the work you do

RESPONSIBILITY/ACCOUNTABILITY: opportunities to be in charge or have control over the outcome of a situation or task

SELF-RESPECT: being able to behave in a way that is consistent with your values

TIME FREEDOM/FLEXIBILITY: having the ability to manage your time as you feel is the most effective

WEALTH: having the potential to accumulate monetary rewards or financial gain

LEADERSHIP: Guiding a group of people or a project; having the opportunity to impact or influence individuals, whether in a formal or informal manner

INTENSITY: an environment that allows for a great deal of emotion and effort

AESTHETIC: the presence of a sense of beauty or an appreciation or concern with the attractiveness of the physical surrounding

AFFILIATION: having a strong sense of belonging, connection, or identification with a group of people or institution

Career Spotlight

MIRANDA PAUL is currently a Visual Merchandising Sales Supervisor at Pandora Jewelry. She graduated from Wingate University with a Bachelor's of Science degree in Business Management and minor in Sociology, and played pitcher on the softball team.

MODULE 9

The Formal Job Market (Applying for Advertised Positions)

There are an astounding number of studies, surveys, and reports on the subject of how the job market actually works to fill open positions, and citing or defending one set of statistics over another is a sure-fire way to get off track from actually looking for a job. One thing, though, is certain: around a quarter to a third of all external hires (as opposed to internal transfers and/or promotions) are brought into the organization by recruiters or other human resources employees who advertise the position externally — primarily through job boards or related electronic means. Applying online is a popular and easy tool for both job seekers and human resources (HR) personnel who are trying to fill jobs. Interestingly, the numbers suggest that applying online is not the BEST way to look for a job (that honor still goes to good old-fashioned networking), but it is a perfectly GOOD way to look, and any good job search plan would include a well-thought-out strategy for applying for open/advertised positions online.

Today, many employers and recruiters are using a specific type of software to support their hiring efforts. These applications are generally referred to as Applicant Tracking Systems (ATS), and their widespread adoption in the last decade has allowed HR departments to automate and store hiring documents online. With ATS systems, recruiters don't have to worry about sifting through stacks of paperwork or hundreds of emails to find what they need any more. As with any technology application, the more you know about how Applicant Tracking Systems work, the greater the likelihood that they'll work in your favor!

53% of former athletes indicated that as undergraduates they knew little to nothing about the hiring process.

Getting Ready to Apply online

Prior to submitting your first online application, there are a few things you will want to do in order to prepare:

1. **HAVE AN ONLINE VERSION OF YOUR RESUME AND COVER LETTER READILY AVAILABLE:** When you apply online, you will have the chance to either "upload" or "copy and paste" your resume into a dialogue box. Because of the many nuances associated with ATS software, most experts recommend that you convert your resume into a separate file just for these purposes. Specifically, when uploading your resume, we recommend you use a Microsoft Word file in a .doc, .txt, or .rtf file rather than the newest version on the market today. Remember, even if you do have access to some of the newest word processing software available, some companies have not made those investments yet — and if they can't read your resume, it doesn't matter how good it is. For similar reasons, we recommend you avoid .pdf files as well; they are harder to manage or manipulate by some ATS systems.

2. **USE KEY WORDS:** Another important feature of an ATS is its ability to scan your resume electronically to look for the specific words that are associated with or describe the skills and experiences that the associated organization is seeking in an ideal candidate. For IT jobs, for example, the recruiting staff may simply program in four or five of the languages or software programs that will be used by the new hire, and they'll run a search through their entire database of resumes looking for those key words or phrases. Knowing this, you can see the logic now in editing and amending your existing resume to reflect the language that you find in the job posting.

3. **DO WRITE A COVER LETTER:** Staffing and recruiting experts are increasingly asserting that cover letters posted online don't get read — and there seems to be some truth to that. Yet, a savvy job seeker covers all bases. If you have done your homework (see Module 13), you can quickly cover this base, and set yourself apart from the competition who didn't take this extra step. Your cover letter should be concise and to the point, specifically addressing the job's requirements. Thoroughly read the job description, edit your resume to include "key words," compose an original cover letter, and make sure your entire application is error free.

Job Board Strategies

While most job boards will differ in one way or another, you should look for the opportunity to do as many of the following as possible:

1. Search for and apply for specific job openings. Of course, this is the foremost reason for their existence in the first place, so most job boards will typically allow you to apply for a job on the site on which you find it. In other cases, the website will redirect you to the home page of the potential employer for this purpose.

2. Post your resume into the system without regard for a specific opening. When you post your resume to the site, the ATS will store your resume for future openings. It will then be able to later search for and review your resume for future openings. This is typically the first place the company will go to look for potential candidates to fill their open positions. In most cases, they will search this database BEFORE they advertise the position, as this is the easiest way to find qualified candidates.

3. Set up a "search agent." Many job boards will allow you to enter a set of criteria that you are interested in — a job title or two, preferred location, and even preferred salary ranges. You can then fill in an email address, and the site will actually send you emails to alert you if a job hits their system that might meet the criteria you entered. A word of caution on this — although this is certainly the easiest method of searching for jobs online, this process is entirely automated and is based only on the key word search strategy mentioned above. These systems certainly can't "think outside the box," so you can count on missing a lot of good opportunities if you don't also visit these sites yourself periodically.

What Sites Should You Use?

As the growth of job-related websites has expanded over the years, it has become increasingly difficult to develop a job search strategy in which the time and energy you put into this piece of the puzzle matches with the results you can expect. If, for example, we assume that 25 to 35 percent of job openings are uncovered online, then smart job seekers will have to create an approach that devotes 25 to 35 percent of their job seeking time to searching for jobs on the web. We recommend that you use the guidelines below (and the accompanying worksheet at the end of this segment) to get organized:

1. **COMPANY HOME PAGES:** As staffing budgets get tighter in many organizations, the HR Department is increasingly turning to their partners in the IT Department to bring this resume management process in-house rather than pay outsiders to do it for them. If you go to a couple of your favorite companies' home pages, you'll almost always find a "Careers" button. To the job seeker, this means that one of the very first ways that companies will advertise a position is on their own site. So, if you have a list of 10-15 companies that you have targeted and really want to work for, your first step is to bookmark those companies "career" pages, and visit them frequently.

2. **JOB SEARCH ENGINES/AGGREGATORS:** Also referred to as meta-search engines, job search engines and aggregators have been around for about 10 years, but they have become powerful tools in the job search sector in recent years. These kinds of search engines "crawl" across the internet and "scrape" off the job opening results they are looking for from various job boards, staffing firms, associations, and company career pages, and aggregate them all onto one site. These sites allow you to view job postings that have been gathered from thousands of potential websites in just a few quick clicks. Top websites in this category include Indeed, Simplyhired, Linkup, Ziprecruiter and Careerjet.

3. **NICHE JOB BOARDS:** A niche job board is a website that focuses its content specifically in one area or category. Most often, these sites are organized around specific industries or job functions (advertising, government, pharmacy, human resources). These sites allow companies to post job openings in a location where targeted candidates can find them in one place. These sites could be an important part of your overall search strategy, because if you locate the boards that focus on the industries or job functions that you are most interested in, then the jobs you find on these sites will be in line with your career interests (and they are all in one place). Another important trend in the niche job board segments are those that are bound geographically rather than by industry, so be sure to explore whether there are sites that are specifically focused on the places you will want to live and work after graduation. A quick Google search will surface a list of top niche boards quickly. You'll want to identify and bookmark the ones that align most closely with your career plans and interests as a next step. A final "niche" board strategy for you will be those sites that tend to focus on recent college grads and entry- level positions.

Aftercollege, Bright, and Collegerecruiter are a few worth looking into as you put this piece of your search strategy together.

4. **THE LARGER GENERALIST ("BIG") BOARDS:** Sites like Monster and CareerBuilder were industry leaders not so long ago, and they continue to have the largest total number of openings of any of the job boards. With the rise of niche boards and aggregators however, these big boards have become a little less popular. Yet, they continue to be a reliable first choice of many advertisers, and any solid search strategy should include at least two of these sites, if not a few more.

5. **SOCIAL MEDIA SITES:** While we'll talk about the benefits of branding and networking via social media sites in Module 10, it is also important to remember that LinkedIn, in particular, is a leading site with regard to advertising/posting specific job openings. Searching the "jobs" function on LinkedIn, along with following your targeted companies on Twitter and Facebook, can also render a number of opportunities. Recruiters are using LinkedIn to view potential candidates for positions they have open, so keep your LinkedIn profile current and error free. Good LinkedIn users want their profiles to be perfect, just like their resume.

External Recruiters/Search Firms

In some cases, employers will seek outside assistance to fill positions; therefore, they will use the services of a recruiter. When a company uses a recruiter, they are essentially hiring a company to go out and find candidates for the employer to interview and hire. While there are a number of different financial arrangements that a recruiter and an employer will enter into to find — or "source" — potential employees, here are a few things to consider if you come into contact with recruiters during the course of your search:

*   In almost all cases these days, if a recruiter presents you to a company who then decides to hire you, the company is expected to pay the recruiter's fees, not you. Usually, recruiters charge the company a fixed percentage (typically 10%–30%) of your first year salary upon hire. If a recruiter asks you to pay a fee for any reason, you should look very carefully before you leap into such an arrangement.

- Recruiters are NOT paid to find YOU a job. They are paid to find an employee for an employer. That is not a subtle difference, so don't be offended if the recruiter doesn't spend a lot of time or energy learning more about your career goals or interests. If you don't fit the profile they are being paid to find, they'll move on quickly.

- Because recruiters do charge a fee to their customer, try not to let a recruiter present your qualifications to a company if you can get in there on your own. Once they do present your qualifications, they get their fee, whether you show up one day or one month later on your own. Who would pay 30% more than list price for the same product if they didn't have to?

> *"Develop a skill that an employer needs and that makes you attractive to recruiters. Learn how to add value and solve a problem or take care of a responsibility for a potential employer, and you will make it a lot easier for someone to hire you."*
> —LAWYER AND FORMER DIVISION I MEN'S TENNIS PLAYER

- Recruiters tend to work in specific professional areas (such as IT, accounting, or engineering), so you'll need to do a little homework to find ones who have a practice area that is connected to the kind of work you are interested in.

- Much as you would if you were applying for a specific job opening, you should write or email a resume and cover letter to any recruiters you decide to include in your overall search strategy. Once you send your resume to a recruiter, remember they can submit it to a long list of potential employers at any time. This may broaden your exposure to the job market and potential employers.

- Some recruiting agencies place employees into limited term "contract" positions. These may be assignments that are 30 to 90 days long only. In some of these cases, there may be an additional "try before you buy" or "temp-to-permanent" contingency. In other words, the employer will elect to try you out on contract for a limited period of time. If things work out, the employer may later hire you directly into the company — or not. In some cases, this can be a good way to get some experience on your resume, and to test-drive an employer at the same time. Remember, you are looking for a workplace that is a good fit for you as well!

Summary

Like many solutions that have gravitated to the Internet in the last several years, there is an ongoing scramble to keep up with the changes and improvements that technology affords us. This is certainly true in the job search game, and by the time you read this text, there may have been even more changes! In order to stay up-to-date with regard to job searching, you'll need to remain keenly aware of the newest methods of uncovering and applying for jobs online. That means understanding how to best format your resume, how the ATS systems work, and which job boards are the most beneficial to you based on your own career interests.

And remember that like so many things, whether seeking employment via responding to advertised positions or working with recruiters, the easiest or fastest way to solve a problem is not always the best way. You'll want to master this reactive aspect of the job search process, but also plan to limit the amount of time you spend searching for a job in this fashion. Remember that the majority of jobs are found through building relationships, as we discuss in the next module.

Career Spotlight

JARIA ATKINS is a Customer Solutions Expert at Blue Cross Blue Shield of North Carolina. She attended North Carolina Central University studying Sports Management and Business and played as a right side hitter for the volleyball team.

EXERCISE

RATIONALE: Many jobs are filled every year though the most traditional ways: employers advertise or post job openings — usually on the Internet — and candidates apply. Yet, with the growth of so many websites and job boards associated with the job search process, you'll need to organize your job search efforts in order to avoid wasting hour after hour on unproductive approaches. The following worksheet is intended to help you uncover the best sites and strategies for you, based on your individual career interests and choices.

EXERCISE 9.1: Online Job Search Strategies

DIRECTIONS: For this exercise, you'll need to select one — and only one — career/occupation, so you can dig as deeply as possible into one job or job family. You can select any career or job title of interest to you for this exercise (e.g., commercial pilot, high school football coach, social worker, nurse, attorney, etc.).

> *Hint: If you're not sure what to choose, you can go back to your Strong Interest Inventory results [see Module 3], and select an Occupation Title from the "Occupational Scales" section that you'd like to learn more about.*

As you go through the questions, you'll need to explore the Web and conduct various Google searches to find what you're looking for. When you see these references *("Indeed. com"; "simplyhired.com")*, or need to identify a major professional association or organization *("ncaa.org")*, just conduct a quick Google search to track these down. As you find them, you might even want to bookmark these sites in your browser for future use!

> *Important Note: In this exercise, we'll be asking you to hunt down a few specific job postings. It will save you a lot of time and energy in the modules to come (specifically Modules 10, 11, and 12) if you print and save three to four of the ones*

that look the most interesting to you. Bookmarking probably won't help, as these jobs could be filled and deleted from the Internet by the time we ask you to use them again.

1. A very rich source of job openings are found directly on the website of the employer or organization for which you want to work. Hunt down 3 of these potential employers, and record the name of the website that their job openings reside on, along with a list of 2 to 3 job openings that they are currently recruiting for:

    Company Name & Website #1 _____
        Job opening: _____
        Job opening: _____
        Job opening: _____

    Company Name & Website #2_____
        Job opening: _____
        Job opening: _____
        Job opening: _____

    Company Name & Website #3_____
        Job opening: _____
        Job opening: _____
        Job opening: _____

2. There are a number of websites that will crawl the web and gather, or "aggregate," job openings by job title and/or geography. Identify 3 aggregators below (hint: we've given you one already), find and list 3 current openings from each of them that are of interest to you and are housed within 100 miles of where you are right now:

Name of aggregator #1 (indeed.com) _____

    Job opening: _____

    Job opening: _____

    Job opening: _____

Name of aggregator # 2 _____

    Job opening: _____

    Job opening: _____

    Job opening: _____

Name of aggregator # 3 _____

    Job opening: _____

    Job opening: _____

    Job opening: _____

3. Many job boards and websites will cater to a specific niche of the job market in order to focus on specific types of jobs and/or locations. Identify 2 such boards that focus on the city/state you live in now, and then 2 more that specialize on the specific kinds of jobs that you identified when you started this exercise:

    Name of two Job Board websites that focus on job openings where you live or want to live:

        1. _____

        2. _____

    Name of 2 Job Board websites that focus specifically on the kinds of jobs you are researching:

        1. _____

        2. _____

4. Finally, the "Big Boards" is where you'll find the highest sheer volume of job openings at any given time, so you'll need to add these to your strategy as well. Try to identify 3 of the biggest job boards on the web today (hint: Google search required), and find 3 more openings on each: (Notice, again, that we've given you a head start by providing you with the first one):

Name of Big Board #1 (monster.com) _____

    Job opening: _____

    Job opening: _____

    Job opening: _____

Name of Big Board #2 _____

    Job opening: _____

    Job opening: _____

    Job opening: _____

Name of Big Board #3 _____

    Job opening: _____

    Job opening: _____

    Job opening: _____

Final note: Did you remember to print 3-4 of the postings you found for later use?

MODULE 10

The Informal Job Market (Networking)

Assume the following: Jim, a 17-year-old locally ranked tennis player moves to a new town, leaving behind all the information and contacts he enjoyed in the local tennis scene. He wakes up on Monday morning, in a new town, and wants to get back in the game. He says to himself, "I want to play some tennis in a solid facility, against good competition, and without paying an arm and a leg to get court time. I sure wish I had more information and knew a few players who could guide me in the right direction." What's your advice to Jim? Would you tell him to act "reactively" by Googling "good tennis?" Look up the names and addresses of all the tennis facilities in town on yellowpages.com and start calling each one? Or would you suggest he behave "proactively", by trying to get in touch personally with some people who might be able to give him face-to-face introductions to tennis pros, facility managers, coaches, or local, top-ranked players? The answer? Both. But, if he were looking for a job instead of some court time, the "proactive" approach would be twice as likely to get him the results he's really looking for.

Jim will get some pretty good info from a "reactive" approach to penetrating the tennis market in this new town, just as you will get some pretty good results by only looking for a job on the Internet. But he is likely get better information, meet people who have similar interests and talents, and find some good players to play with if he gets off the Internet and becomes acquainted with the people who can give him solid information and referrals firsthand. And, he's going to make some new friends who may want to help him based on similar interests and backgrounds.

THAT is how the job market works. Even if companies do advertise some of their job openings on the Web or elsewhere, the majority of job openings are actually filled with people who have been introduced to the hiring team through word-of-mouth or networking, sometimes called the

60% of former athletes indicated that they were rarely to never strategic about growing their networks as undergraduates.

"hidden job market." Yet, even though we all know this intuitively (ask yourself: how did you get your last summer job or internship?), most job-seekers still don't fully employ and leverage the process of developing and actively managing a network of contacts to help them with the job search process.

What is Networking?

At its simplest, networking is developing and managing relationships with people who can help you in your job search by telling you about job leads, offering you advice and information about a particular company or industry, and introducing you to others so that you can expand your network. As an essential component of your job search, your network of contacts are simply a group of people you currently know, along with other people who you will make an effort to get to know (*their* friends) over the course of your job search — and your career. This group will be made up of friends, family, colleagues, coaches, teammates, former teachers, and other people you've met along the way. In short, networking is simply a purposeful process of building and maintaining relationships that may connect you to helpful information or other contacts that also may be able to help.

"I would definitely aim to enlarge my network. I volunteered at Admissions events (such as reunions and meet-ups in large alumni cities) yet never really cultivated my alumni network as much as I should have. I underestimated how much a connection can do for you-- even if it is just moving your resume to the top of the pile."

— Public Relations Specialist and Former Division II Women's Track Athlete

The guiding principal that makes networking so important is this: roughly two-thirds of every hiring decision will be made in favor of a candidate who is somehow known to — or even "friends with" — the hiring company. Only a very few companies set out with a goal to hire a total stranger with no reputation, no track record, or no relationships inside the company — it's just too big a risk. Instead, they want to hire someone whose reputation has been vouched for, someone who will fit in with the culture, or who otherwise has a connection to the firm. Simply put, no one hires a stranger if they can hire a friend instead. So, a critical component of your job search strategy is to build and maintain relationships and make friends with people who have similar career interests as you do.

What Do I Need From My Network

At its simplest, networking is the process of obtaining two very specific things that will move your job search forward:

1. **INFORMATION** on industry trends, market or company intelligence, who's hiring, what employers are really looking for in successful candidates

2. **REFERRALS** to other people, so that you can continue to grow your list of contacts and increase the quality of the information you are gathering as it relates to the kinds of jobs or industries that you are pursuing.

As a first step in the process, you'll need to do a lot of thinking about how your network can help you, so you can communicate clearly to the people you approach. An easy way to get ready for this is by thinking through and taking some notes using the three simple questions listed below. If you can easily talk about this kind of information with the people in your network, then they'll have what they need to truly help you in your career search.

1. Who am I?
2. Where am I going?
3. What help do I need to get there?

Here's an example of what an introductory email to a local high school coach might sound like from a student athlete trying to get her first job coaching women's basketball at the high school or AAU level. Can you pick up how the writer has answered the three questions noted above?

Dear Coach Jones:

We haven't really talked about my plans after graduation, so I wanted to fill you in and also ask for a bit of help from you if you are able to do so. After four years of varsity basketball, I have really developed an interest in working with young people — and specifically younger girls — who are just coming into the more competitive years of basketball. I am exploring career options in this area, perhaps including coaching or running a league in an administrative capacity.

As I try to narrow down these choices, I realize that there is a lot that I know almost nothing about, and this is where I hope you might be able to help. Would you be willing to talk with me for a few minutes about the following:

- *Based on your knowledge of the area, and of women's basketball, can you offer any general advice regarding this idea? Is this a good idea or bad idea?*
- *Can you help me get a better grasp of where the hotbeds of local women's basketball are? Is there a program or organization I should try to connect with? What about at the high school level? Are there other leagues or groups that might be in the very early stages of trying to get started, and might need some help? Or others that are well- established and doing a great job?*
- *Do you know of any specific people here in town who are more deeply involved in girls / women's basketball who you could introduce me to so I could learn a bit more?*

Coach, thanks so much for any help you might be able to give. I will give you a follow up call in the next few days to talk about next steps.

Warm regards,
Betty Basketball Player

How Do I Network?

Networking is often a very informal process. It happens at social events, in classes or libraries, and during tournaments. More often than not, we're all networking all the time. We often make new friends, figure out ways to stay in touch, and exchange texts or stay connected via social media over time. Then, if we want to know something that our friends have information on, we simply ask.

In a job search, though, you'll need to take a more strategic approach to building and maintaining your network to get the information and referrals you'll need in order to get ahead in the world of work. The process includes:

1. Making a preliminary list of your top contacts. There are the people you could easily call on for help without any undue discomfort. The best place to start is with family, friends, coaches, teammates, and others you spend a lot of time with. Then you can work your way out to *their* family, friends, parents of teammates, and neighbors, but that comes later. You'll find a worksheet at the end of this module to help you get started with this exercise.

2. Thinking through what your needs really are with regard to information and referrals, as is reflected in the letter that Betty Basketball wrote. Do you need to know more about a certain industry or company? Do you need a personal referral to someone who knows a lot of about a topic of interest to you? Do you need a contact at a specific company or organization? The important part of this process is to focus first on what YOU need, then on who might be able to help.

3. Planning a good way to let people know of your interest in speaking with them, and specifically what you want to talk about. Then follow up, hoping for a face-to-face meeting, but accepting something less if need be.

4. When you meet, asking good questions, taking good notes, and filing them away for future reference — you'll need them later!

5. Sending a thank you note or acknowledgment of some kind, and agree to let them know about your progress. You don't just want to plant the seeds of a network, you want to water, weed, and feed it over the course of your career!

Bringing Your Network to Life

Looking at your experience on campus as a student-athlete so far, you've very likely, perhaps without even intending to or realizing it, developed a very strong network of contacts. Try this very informal quiz to test this out:

- If you needed help with an injury or illness, who would you contact?

_____

- If you were having a hard time grasping the key concepts in a class, and you were half-way through the semester, who would you call?

  _____

- If your (golf / baseball / tennis / racquetball) swing had been just a bit off in the last few weeks, who would you call?

  _____

- Get your car fixed?

  _____

- Buy a new computer?

  _____

- Get help with a research project?

  _____

- Come up with an idea for a science project?

  _____

- Get a cavity filled?

  _____

For all the questions above that you did NOT know someone directly, would you know who to call to get a referral to someone else who could help?

The point is this: as you enter the working world, of course you'll need to develop a new network, but it will very likely have its roots deeply embedded in the network you already have. The most productive networks — whether formal or informal — will always be made up primarily of *your* friends and *their* friends. And when it comes specifically to looking for a job, the most productive job searches are the ones that rely heavily on the development, care, and feeding of a professional / personal network. Why? Because this is what we know happens when organizations need to fill a job:

- **PEOPLE WILL HIRE PEOPLE THAT THEY ALREADY KNOW AND LIKE.** This is the primary reason behind the statistics that tell us that about two-thirds of jobs are filled via some sort of personal connection. Resumes and cover letters alone — without that personal connection — are just too impersonal to make an employer want to take a chance on you. Not if they don't have to.

- **A WHOLE LOT OF PEOPLE — MOST OF THEM UNQUALIFIED — APPLY FOR JOBS THAT ARE POSTED ONLINE.** This just puts your resume in way too tall of a pile of other resumes. The process of networking puts you into a smaller and more favorable pool of applicants: the "friends of the organization" pool. That's a very different pool than the "anyone with a resume and a computer who happened to see this posting went ahead and applied for it" pool.

- **THE JOB YOU WANT MAY NEVER BE ADVERTISED IN THE FIRST PLACE.** Employers only advertise or post an opening if they have to. While there are a lot of reasons that jobs do get posted, there are a lot more reasons why they DON'T. One of these is very beneficial to networkers: the organization didn't have to post it, because they already knew you, what your interests were, and your current availability. Networking can result in job leads that never get announced to the general public in the first place. This is yet another logical explanation for the "two-thirds of jobs are filled via networking" rule of thumb.

Steps to Effective Networking

Networking is a process, and it requires a game plan. There are lots of ineffective ways to contact your friends and associates, and many of these less effective methods tend to give networking a bad reputation. But with planning, preparation, and some forethought, you can build and maintain a network in your local and professional communities that will help you in any number of ways as you move ahead in your professional career. These steps include:

1. **GETTING FOCUSED:** Networking is most effective when you can:
   a. Easily communicate to others the specifics of your career goals
   b. Identify for others the actual industries, companies, or individuals you are targeting
   c. Develop a specific list of questions that, if answered, can get you the information and referrals that you need to move your job search forward

Without this kind of focus, you'll find yourself stuck with the worst of all networking approaches: the dreaded, "let me know if you hear of anything" request. This approach can in fact do more harm than good, because you'll potentially waste one of the limited numbers of chances you have to leverage someone's desire to help. Responding to requests for specific information, leads, or contacts is much easier for the networking source, and that is your goal: to make the person you're meeting with successful in helping you. Remember, if you don't know what you want out of a conversation, there's no chance that others will.

2. **BUILDING YOUR TOOL KIT:** Before you begin the process of contacting others, you need to put together some of the basic tools of the networking process. These include:

   a. Make sure your **RESUME IS UPDATED** and focused. You should not attach your resume to any initial requests for meetings or conversations, as it is all too easy for others to misunderstand your intentions. When most people see a resume, they automatically think "job application," Good networkers hope job openings surface during the course of their activity, but a resume can get in the way of your primary goal: information, advice, and referrals. Yet, many will ask to see a copy of your resume before the meeting actually takes place. If they ask for one, you need to be able to respond quickly.

   b. As noted above, you should be **FOCUSED ON YOUR INDUSTRIES, COMPANIES, AND PEOPLE OF INTEREST** before you ever ask for a meeting. Better yet, if you can send this information along in your initial request for the meeting, it will show your contact how clearly focused you are, and it will give them some additional time to consider your situation before the meeting. Although each approach letter will be slightly different, you should have a good "information meeting request" template/letter on your computer desktop, ready to be amended and sent out as needed. (See Betty Basketball example in this module.)

   c. Have **BUSINESS CARDS** printed and ready to hand out. You can do this very inexpensively at your local printer or via several easy-to-find websites. You will find that there are a number of situations where handing out a full-blown resume will be inappropriate or awkward, while it is almost always acceptable and easy to hand someone a card to help you contact one another as a follow up. Keep it simple and use just name and contact information. There is no need for target job titles, and unless your goal is to break into the graphic design field, try not to get too fancy.

d. Your **QUESTIONS** for each meeting may vary based on the specific needs you have identified regarding industries, companies, and referrals. Here are a few sample questions to get you started on your own list:

- What experience did you have to get your current position?
- What is your educational background and work experience?
- How much training/supervision did you receive?
- Does your job require you to travel?
- What are the toughest problems and decisions you handle?
- What type of professional and personal skills does it take to succeed at this type of work?
- What is a typical starting salary for someone with my experience?
- What books or journals would you recommend that I read?
- Which professional associations should I join?
- Do you recommend that I enroll in any particular classes?
- What would be a typical next step in the career path for someone in this area after landing an entry-level position?
- What recommendations do you have for me regarding my job search strategy?
- Would you look with me at this list of target companies I have created, and give me some feedback?
- What other people do you recommend that I talk with? May I tell them that you referred me to them?

e. **THANK YOU/FOLLOW-UP NOTES.** While you may opt to use email for much of your job search correspondence, there is still a place in the world of work for tasteful handwritten thank you notes. The person you just met with is busy and has obligations of his or her own that they set aside in order to help you. This is the kind of circumstance that calls for a handwritten note. It shows a touch of class and will set you apart from others in a meaningful way as your network grows. Include your thanks for any specific recommendations and/or referrals that person offered, and offer to keep in touch as your search progresses — and do so! One thing about networking is that you never know where that perfect lead will come from. But it won't come from someone who forgets you're out there looking for a job because you failed to nurture the relationship, that you worked so hard to establish in the first place, with a little common courtesy.

3. **EXPAND YOUR INITIAL LIST OF CONTACTS:** You have probably already considered classmates, teammates, coaches, counselors, and professors. But, have you thought about:

   - Member/officers of the campus alumni organizations?
   - Former employers, including supervisors and coworkers, from summer or part-time jobs?
   - Members of your church, temple, synagogue, or mosque? (Hint: Some larger religious organizations also sponsor job search groups.)
   - Neighbors, both current and past?
   - People you met from political groups or campaigns?
   - Officers or members of professional associations related to your fields of interest?
   - Professionals who provide services to you and your family: attorneys, accountants, doctors, dentists, insurance agents, pharmacists, veterinarians?
   - Relatives, parents of teammates, and friends?

4. **PLAN FOR THE CONVERSATION:** Once you've asked for a meeting or conversation, it is important that you take the initiative and set the agenda in a way that will be fruitful for you, while also respecting the other person's time and commitments. You should ask for no more than 20-30 minutes and then make every effort to stick to that. Ideally, you will have covered some of the following information in an introductory correspondence. However, it is still important that you set a plan for the meeting in such a way that, when you arrive, you'll be able to:

   - Establish rapport and make connections. You should take a moment to catch up on old news, or compare notes on your relationship to the person who referred you, if that is the situation that brought you together. You should also emphasize your gratitude for the meeting, your respect for the person's time and busy schedule and ensure that you are looking for information and referrals, not a job offer.
   - Let the person know as specifically as possible your career goals and plans using this familiar outline:
     a. Where you've been (background, degrees, credentials, volunteer, and professional experience).
     b. Where you hope to land your next job, or what information you need in order to figure that out.

   c. What questions you have that will help you get one step closer to your ulti-
mate goals.

- Ask your questions, take notes, and ask follow up questions.
- Close the meeting with a sincere thank you, an offer to reciprocate in any way that
you may be able to, and a request for permission to stay in touch as your search
progresses.

Networking Tips

Developing and managing a network of personal and professional contacts is one of the key elements of any successful job search. It requires a purposeful approach, and, when executed well, this
effort will be of benefit to both your current job search, and to all aspects of managing your career
for years to come. Along with the guidance offered above, remember to consider the following:

- One reason many students fail to network is because they ask themselves: "Why would
anyone take the time out of their busy day to help me?" It's a good question, but with a
pretty straightforward answer: People like to help. It feels good. And almost everyone
today knows just how it feels to be looking for work. We've all done it, and we all have
some level of expertise in it. People like giving advice, and they like to be recognized for
their expertise. As long as that's what you're asking people to do, they'll do it willingly and
happily. If you make it a chore for them, however, it will not go nearly as well. You need to
be seen as the one who owns the process, not your contact.

- Networking is about asking for advice and referrals, not for a job. Asking for a job puts a lot
of pressure on the other person in the room, and you want your contacts to become allies
in your job search, not make them feel uncomfortable by their inability to help. Almost no
one can give you a job, but almost everyone can give you advice that will help.

- Be specific in what you ask for. Before you go off and reconnect with everyone you've ever
met, do your homework. How can this person be helpful to you at this time? Do you need
a reference? An insider's take on an industry? A referral? An introduction to someone in
the field?

- Finally, be prepared to reciprocate. Look for ways to help others as much and as often as
they help you. Before you close any meeting or conversation, ask, "Now what can I do to
help you?" If you run across other interesting information while you're on the journey, send

it along to those who would also find it interesting. If you meet others you think would benefit from each other, make the introduction. Building a network is a lot like gardening. Turning over the dirt and planting seeds at the beginning of the process is the hardest part, but it's not the only part. You'll still have to weed, water, and fertilize it over time to get the harvest you're looking for.

Social Media

While it may come as a surprise to members of your parents' generation, today's college students and recent graduates will not be a bit alarmed to read that 93% of recruiters use social media as a tool for recruiting candidates. In fact, many recruiters and hiring managers take a fair amount of pride in their ability to seek out great job candidates on social media, making the online environment one in which there is a dramatic increase in activity and traffic (Jobvite, 2015).

Today, we no longer question *whether* to include a social media strategy into a job search, but question what is the most efficient and effective way to include this strategy. Social media tools can help you research and follow targeted companies and industries, contact alumni or friends who work at your target companies, engage in professional conversations in your areas of vocational interest, and apply for job openings, all via your keyboard, tablet, or smart phone. Although the uses of social media are practically limitless these days, the savvy job seeker should, at minimum, create a plan to use these web-based tools to:

- Make connections and build your network, both with those you know and have interacted with in the past, and those people your current contacts can connect you with. You should place special emphasis on those contacts you already know or have interacted with at school or in work settings who can connect you to the industries, organizations, and companies that you are targeting in your job search.

- Join groups related to your areas of interest. Be an active contributor to their discussions, with an emphasis on identifying specialty groups within your specific area of interest, campus alumni groups, or professional associations. When you contribute to discussions, remember that your every word will be scrutinized by potential employers, so make sure that your grammar, tone, and content is flawless.

Hint: Sometimes you can find good groups to join by finding out what groups other people in your network or classes have joined.

- Research specific companies that are on your target list (and their competitors) to learn about the culture, any potential new initiatives that may create a need to hire, and specific hiring/ recruiting practices within these potential places of employment.
- Learn more about the industries and markets that tend to hire people with your background and career interests.
- Identify information about and apply for specific job openings.

Although there are hundreds of social media websites and apps on the web today, you will find it useful to narrow your focus to the three that are most widely used by both job seekers and recruiters: LinkedIn, Facebook, and Twitter. While it is very likely that you have already been using at least one, if not all three of these sites, we'll examine (or revisit) each of them here from an introductory standpoint, with a specific emphasis on job search and career management applications.

LinkedIn

LinkedIn is a social networking site designed specifically for the business community. The site's goal is to allow its members to establish networks of people they know and trust professionally. Basic membership is free to all registered users. After signing up, a LinkedIn member first creates a profile page, which emphasizes employment history, education, and other factors associated with work history, experience and education. With basic membership, you can then establish a "connection" with someone you competed with, worked with, know professionally (online or offline), or attended school with. The beauty of LinkedIn is that, every time you add someone to your personal network, you'll get access to his or her connections as well. You will also have access to the networks of each of those people. Members of their network become your second and third-level connections, and, with the addition of these people, you will see your number of connections grow well beyond your immediate list of contacts very quickly. So, LinkedIn users from all over the world can join the site for free, create a profile that showcases their professional skills and history, and network with other users with whom they are connected.

For job seekers, this provides you access to people at a vast number of companies, along with the ability to view and join the personal networks of others. These factors make LinkedIn a goldmine of potential chances to research companies, establish personal connections, and get access to job openings that others might never see. To get started or to enhance your LinkedIn profile and strategy, you should:

1. **BUILD YOUR PROFILE:** Your LinkedIn profile will capture much of the same information as your resume, so you can "double-dip" by including most of the information in your resume here as well. This profile will be in many ways the equivalent of a resume that is posted online, and it will help your contacts better understand your career goals and interests. Much like your resume, your profile should contain information regarding your past positions, accomplishments, specialties, and recommendations from other professional contacts. As an added benefit, it will also be available to the hundreds — if not thousands — of recruiters who search LinkedIn constantly in search of candidates for open or upcoming jobs.

    Hint: Remember that recruiters often search for potential candidates by keywords in LinkedIn profiles, so be sure — as you did with your resume — to use keywords and phrases that may be used by a recruiter or hiring manager to find someone with your skills.

2. **BEGIN TO BUILD AND/OR GROW YOUR LIST OF CONTACTS:** A network of connections is a crucial part of your LinkedIn usage — both the size and strength of your network is important. As you build your network, invite people you know from your athletic pursuits, of course, along with fellow students in your areas of vocational interest, coaches, past employers, mentors, school or volunteer organizations, and others from your personal network.

3. **SEEK OUT AND APPLY FOR EXISTING JOB OPENINGS THAT ARE POSTED ON THE SITE:** LinkedIn operates a straightforward job board with openings that can come from a variety of sources. These positions can be posted directly by an organization, individuals, recruiters, or they can come from any number of LinkedIn's many business partners, who can pay a fee to advertise/post openings on this job-related site. LinkedIn is one of the top sources of openings posted to the web, and using this function to locate and apply for openings should be an integral part of your overall search strategy.

4. **JOIN AND PARTICIPATE IN A FEW LINKEDIN GROUPS:** Joining groups is an important way to build your network and to get noticed by others in the hiring community. Because both employers and recruiters frequently join and participate in groups that have members with common professional interests, you can get noticed by recruiters by participating in discussions or sending them a personal message that indicates your career and job search goals. Often such groups will operate and maintain a group job board as well, so don't let those opportunities escape your attention.

Facebook

Although most of us continue to think of Facebook as a social site rather than a professional one, recruiters are now turning their attention to Facebook to look for and research candidates for job openings. With this, the first strategy for college graduates entering the job market is to "scrub" your existing Facebook profile in such a way that you eliminate any information that might not present you in the most professional light. Be sure to modify your Facebook profile to convey a professional tone and manner. Assume that your profile will be viewed by business professionals and other important contacts, so only include information that

> 50% of former athletes indicated that they rarely to never worried about managing their brand or reputation as undergraduates.

supports your professional reputation. For example, if you majored in Sports Administration, and enjoyed coaching Little League, you should indicate this interest in your profile.

Next, you should fill out your profile with a professional history, using the "Work and Education" section. Again, with all the work you've already done to build out your resume and LinkedIn profile, you won't need to start from scratch. A clever "copy-and-paste" job should take care of this challenge in a matter of minutes — although, on Facebook, you'll probably want to use a shorter version of the information that you have already created.

As with LinkedIn, you can type in the names of your target companies in the search bar and then identify those members of your network (your "friends") who work at that those companies. You can also use Facebook to find out more about target companies by viewing their Facebook profiles. If your target companies have Facebook pages, be sure to "like" them. You can also find and pursue actual job opportunities, either on a company's Facebook page, or by visiting the "Marketplace" section, where you can search for openings by category, job title, industry, company, location, and more.

Twitter

Finally, Twitter is an online social networking service that allows friends — and sometimes employees and companies — to communicate through the exchange of quick (140 characters or less) messages, called "Tweets." These short messages are posted to the writer's profile and sent to their followers as well. Everyone's updates are also searchable via both a Twitter search and through a Google search. Although Twitter appears to be the least utilized of the social media sites for job seekers, you should take a few minutes to ensure that you're not passing up the chance further develop your social media job search strategy by using this very popular site. In addition to composing a tweet, you can search Twitter for just about anything, including jobs.

A few ways to take advantage of Twitter in a job search include:

1. You can follow the activity of targeted employers, companies, or organizations. Many organizations establish a Twitter presence to keep their brands and services in the public eye.

2. You can identify the people at these companies that are specifically engaged in the hiring process, including recruiters. If you are able to identify such individuals, you can follow their activities to see if they are tweeting about job openings or hiring plans for the future.

3. Also, as with Facebook, you may want to build (or rebuild) your profile to reflect your professional/vocational goals rather than your personal interests and activities.

4. You can also use hashtags in the Twitter search box in a few specific and targeted ways:
    a. For example, you can find job advice and listings through hashtags like #jobs, #recruiting, #jobadvice, #jobposting, #jobhunt and #jobsearch.
    b. Also, any industry conferences and other professional gatherings or association activities will have their own hashtags.

Finally, remember that in all social media applications, you are building a personal brand online with every activity you engage in, so be sure that your presence represents you as a professional.

Summary

We learned that there are a number of tools that employers have at their disposal to fill open positions. Many of those tools and practices have moved to a technology platform, so you will have to learn, and keep up with, the trends related to the newest job boards, the programming nuances that underlie resume management software, and how to make your resume accessible to web-based technologies, since, as you now know, about a third of jobs are filled in this way. Yet, you will want to adopt a job search strategy — both now and after graduation — that can be 100% efficient. To pick up the remaining two-thirds of the job market, you will need to add a solid and efficient networking strategy to your career plan.

As your career planning process unfolds and develops, you should find yourself moving from "what do I want to do?" to "how do I get there?" A key component to that latter question is understanding how the job market works and putting a game plan into place that reflects that awareness.

As you begin to formulate your networking strategy, keep the following driving principles in mind:

- Networking, when done well, relies equally on the warm handshakes and on the savvy utilization of online networking in both business and personal settings. Don't rely too heavily on either the value of a personal connection or the tools available online. To be most effective, stay connected to others, and keep on top of your virtual brand.

- Very rarely will any employer or organization go out and hire a total stranger — unless they have no alternative whatsoever. That means that the more friendships and relationships that you can develop among those who make hiring decisions — or those who make recommendations to hiring authorities — the more likely you are to get the job you've set your sights on.

- To network effectively, you have to take the steps necessary to put your friends and colleagues in a position where they know HOW to help you. That means you have to know what you want, where you're going, and how they can help you get there. If you can't be specific in what you need — you haven't done your homework yet. So go do it. And let them know clearly how they can help.

- A network, when built with integrity, will last you a lifetime. It should not be seen as different or apart from your friendships. The best network contacts, in fact, will always be your friends and their friends. You should be prepared to maintain these relationships throughout your search and beyond, and to provide this same kind of help to others when asked.

- Some people say, when it comes to the job market, that it's "not what you know, it's who you know." As this program demonstrates, being a solid manager of your own career takes a little more than that, but when it comes to networking — that theory is not all wrong!

Career Spotlight

PEACE SHEPARD EASTON is currently working as a Health Service Specialist at Aetna Health Insurance and she's the girls' basketball varsity head coach of Holly Springs High School. Peace graduated from North Carolina State University with a Bachelor's of Arts degree in Sociology. She played basketball for legendary coach Kay Yow, and was a member of the 1998 Final Four team.

EXERCISES

RATIONALE: Like most of us, you have likely made many connections with people throughout your life, whether it be through your athletic endeavors, your home/community, at school, or elsewhere. You probably remain connected more closely to some of your friends and contacts than others, and you likely have forgotten about others with the passage of time. The exercise below will remind you of the many people you have met along the way who might be instrumental to helping you reach your career goals in the future. Making this list now, by referring to any and all of the various ways that you are connected with them (Facebook, college projects, etc.), will pay big dividends later, when your networking efforts will begin in earnest. Of course, you should continue building this list throughout your college career.

EXERCISE 10.1: **Building Your Professional Network**

DIRECTIONS: List your current and past contacts under each of the categories below, emphasizing those that might be able to support you in meeting your career and professional goals.

Family	Friends
Teammates	Teammates' Parents
Coaches/Former Coaches	Athletic Administrators

Fraternity/Sorority	Volunteer Organizations
Religious Organizations	Professors
Academic Advisors	Young Alumni in Workplace
Guest Speakers	Past/Present Employers
Student Organizations and Clubs	On-Campus Recruiting/Job fairs

EXERCISE 10.2: Networking Approach Email Template (See Betty Basketball)

RATIONALE: While you have spent some time in this module learning about networking, how it works, and how you can use a networking strategy to enhance your career exploration, others may have no idea what you are trying to accomplish when you approach them. To be effective in this networking role, you have to be able to educate others on how to help you. This exercise — in which you are asked to draft a letter/email to someone in your network to ask for their support — is designed to get you thinking about how you will communicate your goals and your need for information and referrals to others. Remember, it's not enough that YOU know what you're trying to accomplish via networking, THEY have it understand it too.

DIRECTIONS: Compose a networking approach email using the three questions below as a guide / outline. Use the letter by Betty Basketball in this module as a guide, and focus on answering the three questions below as an outline.

1. Who am I? (Career-related degrees or courses, skills, experience, credentials, background)

    _____

    _____

    _____

    _____

2. What am I interested in learning more about or doing next?

    _____

    _____

    _____

    _____

3. How can this person help?

    _____

    _____

    _____

    _____

MODULE 11
Interview Basics

Prior to a game, the best coaching staffs will have prepared a detailed scouting report. In it they generally address these three key components:

1. What kind of shape are we in as a team for this week's game? What are our strengths and weaknesses? Is our first string point guard out with a high ankle sprain? Do we have key players out on academic suspension? Has our team free throw shooting percentage gone up in recent weeks?

2. What does the other team look like? Does their starting pitcher rely on first pitch strikes? Does their football team run the ball on the first three possession of every game? Is their anchor really the faster runner on their team?

3. Where are the key match-ups? Is our center four inches taller than theirs? How do our bats line up against their bullpen? How many curve ball pitchers vs. first pitch fast ball hitters do they have? How much better is our anchor swimmer than theirs?

As in sports, in order to win at the interview game, you'll need to prepare yourself in three ways. You'll have to assess your own skills, credentials, and experiences; you'll have to assess the prospective employer's business model and employment needs; and you'll need to see how your resume and experiences match up with the employer's current and future plans and needs. If you take this kind of approach to interview preparation, you can win the job offer!

With this in mind, let's take a look at the key issues associated with the interview process, from start to finish: ways to prepare yourself **before** the interview, key issues and questions that will likely come up **during** the interview itself, and how to follow-up **after** the interview.

Before the Interview

RESEARCH: In order to win in the game of interviewing, you'll need to do some research on both the company and the specific job position before you ever show up. At minimum, you should carefully review the organization's website and look for articles about the organization in major periodicals or industry trade journals. You will want to know as much as possible — more than the other interviewees do — about the company's mission statement, values, and history, before moving on to learn about the products or services they offer, who some of their bigger clients are, and who their biggest competitors are. If you have the connections (on LinkedIn or Facebook, for example) you can also talk with a handful of the company's current employees as well. You should go above and beyond your competition in this investigation, as this is one of the clearest ways you can demonstrate to the interviewer and others at the company how committed you are to winning the interview competition.

REVIEW THE JOB POSTING CAREFULLY — AGAIN AND AGAIN: What are the top three specific skills, experiences, and interests you can offer this specific employer? Identify them by comparing your background specifically against the job posting, and then determine how you'll communicate your skills to the prospective employer when answering interview questions. When possible, tell stories from your background that matches up with the needs you've identified in the posting. Even when you don't have specific transferable skills for some aspects of the job, remember that you should still have stories that demonstrate that you are quick learner, that you are committed to finishing tasks that you start, or are a recognized team player. Remember, these strengths too are a part of a younger worker's profile. If you're interviewing for an entry- level role against others with similar levels of experience, the employer may be looking just as much at your potential to learn as your ability to come in and hit the ground running. Being prepared to address these less tangible strengths and personality traits can go a long way.

PREPARE EXAMPLES: Think about actual stories (see Module 4) you can tell from your previous experience to support your candidacy for the job. The interviewer will want to see how your current skills fit with the requirements of the job, and the best way to accomplish that is to tell stories about your previous achievements. Remember, most interviewers are trained to believe that anything that you've actually done before is the best predictor of whether you can do it again — for them after you are hired. Why? Because demonstrating that you've actually done the work in the past is more convincing than just saying you can do it. Make sure your stories are appropriate, interesting, and to the point, and that you know them inside and out.

> **Tip**: *You can actually bring a list of these stories with you to the interview, as long as they are in a professional looking portfolio or binder. You should also consider bringing a few extra copies of your resume, a pen, and an 8½ x 11" pad of paper. You should plan on handing your resume to anyone that has not seen it.*

DEVELOP INTELLIGENT QUESTIONS: Most interviewers will save five minutes or so at the end of the interview to ask you if you have any questions for them. The right answer to that request is, "Yes, I do. Thank you for giving me that opportunity." (The WRONG answer is, "No I think you've explained everything perfectly.") There are two issues in play here: one is your chance to show genuine interest in the role, and the other is to show that you have prepared more than your competition to generate really thoughtful questions that will engage the interviewer/interview team in a conversation with you.

"Student-athletes should form a plan for job interviews. The interview is the selling point and very important. If you are not prepped, it could be a disaster. Play up the skills learned and challenges faced by student-athletes. Also, diversify your experiences so you can tell non-sports related stories and you seem more well- rounded"

—Paralegal and Former Division II Women's Swimmer

This is your chance to demonstrate your level of interest in the job and to show how seriously you took the preparation for the interview itself. If, for example, your research demonstrates that the stock price of the company has fallen steadily in the last 90 days, and also that the company has been building a new plant in Tennessee, you might ask something like, "I see that your stock has taken a bit of a drop in value recently. Do you think that is tied to your new expansion plans, or is there something else going on in the marketplace?"

Below is a list of some of the more typical questions that candidates ask in interviews. You should use these as a starting point rather than as final products. You should plan to edit and amend these based upon the results of your research rather than using them word-for-word.

- *What is a typical career path for someone hired into this position?*
- *Can you tell me more about how employees are evaluated in the performance review process?*
- *If I were to be hired, what are the departmental priorities when I come on board?*
- *Will I receive any training or mentorship for this position? If so, for how long?*
- *What should a person in this position focus most on accomplishing in the first two or three months?*
- *What do you like most about working with this company?*
- *How would you describe the culture at this company?*
- *What is the next step in your hiring process?*
- *Can I send you any other information to help with your decision?*
- *What would you say is the greatest challenge in this job?*
- *How do you rate your competition?*
- *What is a normal day like for a person who holds this position?*
- *What types of projects or job assignments would I be asked to handle?*
- *What are the biggest challenges of this job?*
- *What are the most important elements of this job?*
- *What goals do you expect the person who takes this job to achieve during the first year (or 30, 60, or 90 days)?*
- *If I was starting in this position today, what would you advise me to learn first and do first?*
- *What opportunities do you make available for professional development and training?*
- *Are there any reservations you have about my fit for the position that I could try to address?*
- *What is the next step in this process?*
- *What is your timeline for getting back to candidates about the next steps?*
- *What are the three main factors you will be using to determine the right person for this job?*
- *What did the last person in this position go on to do — and what was their background?*

SELECT WHAT TO WEAR: In an interview, you will need to dress professionally. Invest some time to put together a dark-colored business suit or a jacket and matching pants or knee-length skirt. Make sure you feel comfortable and confident in what you're wearing. Do not to wear sneakers, tennis shoes, sandals, or any open-toed shoes. Above all, do not wear a t-shirt or jeans to an interview. You only get one opportunity to make a first impression.

KNOW WHERE YOU'RE GOING: You cannot be late for interviews — period. Get there at least 15 minutes in advance. Get good directions to the company ahead of time, and if you can, practice traveling to the site. Don't trust your GPS this time.

During the Interview:

BE READY FOR "TMAY" (TELL ME ABOUT YOURSELF") RIGHT OUT FOR THE GATE. Referred to sometimes as your "elevator speech," or the "90-second commercial," this is often the first question in an interview. It is a really good ice breaker for both of you, and it gives you a chance to kick off the interview in a positive way. If you're ready for it, that is. In some less scripted interview formats, what you say in response to this standard question can actually influence the next questions during the interview in a positive way. Keep your response under two minutes, and make sure that it connects with the needs of the position.

As you prepare your answer, think about including your degrees and credentials, some of your favorite recent experiences, why you chose this major/their industry to explore, and most importantly, how and why you think you can help them achieve their goals as a future employee. If it fits the format and the mood in the room, you should try to finish your response with a question of your own, in an effort to transform this "interrogation" into a give- and-take discussion. You can close with something like, "Are there any specific aspects of my background that you'd like me to spend a little more time on at this moment?"

In any case, this is your first and best chance to show them that you are very clear on who you are, what you want from your career, and what value you can offer their organization. Remember to stay in control of what you can control, and that is how you feel, look, and respond to questions. So — be ready!

BE READY FOR OTHER QUESTIONS: There are, of course, a lot of very common interview questions. A list of the most common ones are found at the end of this module. You should certainly read this list carefully, but trying to memorize a list of 50 answers to 50 questions in advance will probably hurt you more than help you. Instead, you should have a strategy that will help you anticipate or respond on the fly to all questions. A few pieces of advice include:

- A whole family of questions, often called "behavioral" questions, rely on an interviewing strategy of trying to get you to tell actual stories from your training, education, and experiences. You will recognize these if you're aware of the strategy, as they will all be phrased in a similar way, in that the attempt is to get you to "tell me a story." Thus, the beginning of these questions will start with: "Tell me about a time when…"; "When was the last time you…"; or "Can you give an example of a time when you…" So, as pointed out earlier (and will be covered again in more detail in Module 12), be prepared for these types of questions by thoroughly analyzing your background and develop "stories" that point out your skills and qualities.

- Use as much of your attention and focus as you can muster to REALLY listen and respond directly to the questions that are asked. If, after you've heard the question, you just come up totally blank, you can always ask the interviewer to repeat it. That will show that you're fully present in the interview and give you some valuable time to think and re-group.

- When you think you really don't have a good answer to a question, don't apologize or offer excuses for shortcomings. Instead, emphasize your willingness to learn new things and develop these skills. Similarly, when asked the "weakness" or "shortcomings" question, own up to it. Of course, you have a lot to learn. The only way you can really hurt yourself here is by coming off as defensive or uncomfortable. If they had a candidate with every single qualification for the job, they wouldn't be talking to you!

EMPLOY GOOD BODY LANGUAGE STRATEGIES: Start your interview by greeting the interviewer with a smile and a firm handshake. Maintain eye contact at all times. Make eye contact with all members of an interview panel, with special emphasis on the one that asked the question when they alternate. Don't squirm around in your chair, pull on your hair, or fiddle with your fingers.

CLOSE THE INTERVIEW WITH STRENGTH. Don't forget to be ready with those questions that you have prepared for the interviewers. Also think about forming new questions over the course of the interview that will bring out additional information on any of the more interesting topics that came up during the interview. Be sure to use these final exchanges of conversation and information as a chance to repeat how this position and/or the organization are a good match for you. If you think it makes sense, you can also ask if they have any concerns about your candidacy for the job after today's discussion, as you would certainly want to address any reservations while you have the chance. And, don't leave the room without asking when they expect to make a decision and/or let you know about next steps in the process. Finally, try to get contact information on everyone you met, so you can follow up appropriately after the interview is concluded.

Below is a brief list of commonly asked interview questions:

- Tell me about yourself.
- What are your top three strengths?
- What are your top three weaknesses?
- Why do you want this job?
- Where would you like to be in your career five years from now?
- What attracted you to our company?
- Why should we hire you?
- What do you know about this industry?
- What do you know about our company?
- Are you willing to travel? If so, how much?

After The Interview

Even though the interview is over, the hiring *process* isn't. Although you are now headed home, the interviewer and his or her team or committee is still on the job. Although you can't see it from the outside, the team will soon be filling out evaluation forms on all the candidates that they met, and they'll meet as a group to discuss and share their impressions of each candidate. In many cases, this process can go on for another several weeks — leaving you time to continue to compete for the offer! Since the game is still on, below are a few recommendations for the follow-up phase of the interview process.

TAKE SOME NOTES: As soon as it is practical, find a quiet time to sit down and record your observations, recollections, and questions about the interview. You'll need this information specifically to write good follow-up notes to the interviewing team, to prepare for the next round of interviews, and to evaluate more clearly any potential job offer. As you take your notes, pay special attention to the following:

- Do you have the full names and contact information for each interviewer?
- Do you know the department of each member of the interview team (HR, Marketing, Operations)?
- Can you list any specific questions or concerns that each interviewer expressed?

- What did you learn about each interviewer?
- What did you learn about this industry/company?
- Did you learn anything that either confirmed or modified your interest in this job or career path?

SEND THANK YOU NOTES: Although there is a great deal of discussion today about the best way to follow-up with thank you notes after an interview, there is NO debate on whether or not it is a critical part of the process. You must send follow-up notes to each individual you met — no duplicates. Whether it is an email or a written thank-you note, this kind of follow-up is a hallmark of professionalism. These thank you notes should, at minimum, thank the people who interviewed you for time and interest, inform them of your continued interest in the role, let them know that you look forward to hearing from them, and tell them they should not hesitate to let you know if you can answer any more questions.

> **Tip:** *If you were presented initially to the company by an outside recruiter or agency (see Module 10), be sure also to follow up with a phone call to the recruiter and ask how the interview went and what next steps you should take.*

IF YOU DO NOT GET THE JOB, LOSE GRACEFULLY: While no one likes losing, it takes a lot of class to lose in a way that might just set you up for a win down the road. You should write a second thank you note if this happens, letting the interviewer know that, while naturally you were disappointed to learn that you were not the top choice, you still retain a great deal of interest and enthusiasm for the company. Let the employer know that you'd be happy to be considered for opportunities that might surface in the future. Remember, the organization liked you enough to bring you in in the first place. This could simply be a case of you being almost the right fit this time — but the perfect fit next time.

Summary

In this module, we've introduced you to the basics of interviewing. With this information, you can begin to think about the kinds of questions you'll need to be ready for, and, more importantly, the kind of preparation you'll need to do in order to compose and deliver the kind of solid answers that will win you offers. It is important to remember that:

1. When the interview and selection process is working most effectively, both parties — the company and you — are doing their part. Hiring managers should have already thought through what kinds of skills, experiences, and credentials they want in an ideal candidate, and the interviewee should have already reviewed his/her skills, experiences, and credentials as well. The interview itself — that critical 30–60-minute period — is when the two parties can compare and contrast the results of all this preparation together. In other words, the company has probably already done their homework. You'll be at a big disadvantage if you haven't done yours.

2. Getting ready for interviews works best when you plan on action steps for each of the three specific periods: before the interview, during the interview itself, and after the interview. Each has its own requirements, characteristics, and purposes. If you can take each one of these challenges on in its own time and place, you have a solid chance of winning the interviewing game.

Career Spotlight

SHANA HARTMAN is currently Associate Professor of English at Gardner-Webb University. She graduated from East Carolina University with a Bachelor's of Arts degree in English education, and played defense for the women's soccer team.

EXERCISE

RATIONALE: Just as in any game or match you've ever participated in as an athlete, you know better than most the value of research and preparation. Employers want to know that you have given meaningful thought not only to YOUR vast array of talents, strengths, and skills, but that you've focused considerable attention on THEIR needs and business challenges as well. The following worksheet is a hands-on reminder of the kind of research that you can, and should, conduct in advance of any job interview. If you can complete most of this worksheet before you show up at the interview, you'll be better equipped than most of your competition to win a job offer.

EXERCISE 11.1: Interview Prep Checklist

DIRECTIONS: Find an open job from any job board or other source that you would be interested in competing for if you were currently looking (or use one of those you identified in Module 9). Now assume you have been scheduled for an actual job interview with that organization. Using the worksheet below, prepare for your "interview" with this company.

Company Information

Employer Name:

_____

Address:

_____

Position Interviewing for:

_____

Name and Title of Interviewer(s):

_____

Date and Time of Interview:

_____

Directions to the Interview:

_____

_____

Company Research

Key Information from Company Homepage:

_____

_____

_____

Industry Trends:

_____

_____

Key Competitors:

_____

_____

Percentage of Market Share:

_____

Current Contacts Connected to the Company:

_____

_____

Social Media Presence/News (Facebook, Twitter, LinkedIn):

_____

_____

Your Value

Key strengths relevant to job description

1. _____

2. _____

3. _____

3-5 key stories to sell your abilities and skills (See Module 4)

1. _____

2. _____

3. _____

4. _____

5. _____

Questions you want to ask

1. _____

2. _____

3. _____

4. _____

5. _____

Items to Bring to Interview
- Portfolio with paper & pen
- Job Description
- Resumes for each interviewer
- Questions for interviewer
- Project samples (if applicable)

Career Spotlight

SHANNON MCGINLEY is currently the Founder & CEO of CityShape Fitness. CityShape is a premiere fitness pass in Kansas City offering members one membership to multiple fitness studios around the city, eliminating the need to commit to one type of workout. CityShape aims to change Kansas City's fitness landscape. Shannon graduated from the the University of Kansas with a Bachelor's of Science degree in Business Marketing, and played left field for the KU softball team.

MODULE 12
Behavioral Interviewing

Your softball team is headed into the first round of the conference tournament. It's a "win or go home" format. There are two scouting reports available to you on the opposing team. Which one do you want?

1.   Their leadoff hitter is really fast, and their clean — up hitter pounds the ball.

or

2.   Their leadoff hitter has stolen 36 bases in 45 attempts during the regular season. Their fourth hitter hit .367 during the regular season over 67 games, and .388 with runners in scoring position. She hit .38 points higher off left-handed pitching, and hasn't bunted all season.

Most players are going to go with the second scouting report. Why? Because it's an objective, factual, and numbers-driven recap of the player's actual performance in past game situations. Given the difficult task of predicting any team's performance on the playing field in a future game against an unknown opponent, a player's — and a team's — past performance in previous game situations is the single best tool we have to try to decide how to approach the game.

The idea that the best predictor of events that may occur in the future lies in what has happened in the past has been around for quite a while in the world of sports. In more recent years, it has taken hold in the world of interviewing as well, and today, almost all organizations have trained their recruiters and hiring managers to adopt such an interviewing strategy. It is most frequently

70% of former athletes indicated that they knew little to nothing about how to effectively answer Behavioral Interview questions as an undergraduate.

referred to as *"Behavioral Interviewing,"* or *"competency-based interviewing."* Today, many companies have gone so far as to develop manuals, worksheets, scoring templates, sample questions, and all sorts of materials to support this type of interviewing strategy.

In baseball, it's easier to get on base if you know what's coming. The same is true of interviewing. In order to hire the right person for the future of the company, hiring managers are going to want to know as much as they can about the candidate's past work-related behaviors and activities. The following section is your scouting report to help you get ready for the game of behavioral interviewing!

What is Behavioral Interviewing?

Behavioral interviewing is a specific interview technique in which job candidates are asked questions designed to force them to give the interviewer concrete examples of how they have performed in the past during certain situations. This type of interview question is intended to help the interviewer understand how this person will perform in the specific job they are interviewing for. Because behavioral interviewing is based on the theory that a person's pattern of performance does not change significantly over the course of their adult life, their past behavior is a solid indicator, or predictor, of how they will perform in similar situations in the future.

"Prepare for the types of interviews (behavioral) that are being used in today's job market. I see/hear a lot of the same interview questions today as I did when I was participating in mock interviews as a college student. Also, take notes when doing these mock interviews. I still have mock interview notes from my freshman year in college that I go back and look at before a job interview."

—Audit Manager and Former Division III Baseball Player

Once again — the idea is simple — and worth repeating. Your ability to answer these kinds of questions in the best possible way requires you to fully adopt the first premise that guides the whole process: *the most accurate predictor of future performance of a potential employee is that person's past performance in similar situations.*

The interviewer's goal is to get you to tell them about your own career-related experiences, behaviors, knowledge, skills, and abilities that the company has decided are desirable in a particular position.

Here is a list of commonly asked behavioral interview questions:

- *Tell me about a time when you had to motivate yourself.*
- *Tell me about a time you had to effectively work under pressure.*
- *Tell me about a time when you made a mistake. How did you handle it?*
- *Tell me about a goal that you set for yourself that you achieved.*
- *Tell me about a decision that you made that was not popular. How did you handle it?*
- *Tell me about a time you successfully worked on a team.*
- *Tell me about a time when you disagreed with someone at work. How did you handle it?*
- *Share an example of how you were able to motivate those around you.*
- *Give me an example of a goal that you set that you didn't meet. How did you handle it?*
- *Tell me about a time when you made a risky decision? Why did you do it?*
- *Tell me about a time when you went above and beyond the call of duty? How and why did you do it?*
- *Tell me about a time when you had to work on more than one project at a time. How did you decide on what to work on first?*
- *Tell me about the last tight deadline that you had to meet.*
- *Tell me about a situation where you were able to successfully persuade someone to see things your way.*
- *Tell me about a time when you had to conform to a policy with which you did not agree. How did you handle it?*
- *Tell me about a time you were able to successfully work with another person even when you did not personally like that individual or vice versa.*
- *Tell me about a time when you took the lead on a project. What did you do?*
- *Tell me about a recent situation in which you had to deal with a very upset customer or co-worker.*
- *Tell me about a time when you set your goals or expectations too high or too low.*

How Do Companies and Other Organizations Prepare for Behavioral Interviews? (The Other Teams' Game Plan)

This is what the well-prepared companies do to set up their internal behavioral interviewing programs:

1. Identify some of the key "competencies," or qualities that the company has decided are desirable for its employees to possess. Typically, companies will have identified a long list of these competencies that can apply across all departments or divisions within the organization, but the interviewing team that you will meet with will probably select four to six competencies from that master list to apply to the job in question. Examples of these competencies may include:

   - Accountability
   - Analytical Thinking
   - Building Trust
   - Change Management
   - Customer Focus
   - Entrepreneurship
   - Fiscal Management
   - Getting Results
   - Influencing Others

   - Interpersonal Skills
   - Managing Performance
   - Negotiating
   - Organizational Communications
   - Partnering/Networking
   - Project Management
   - Technology Use/Management
   - Valuing and Leveraging Diversity
   - Innovation

2. Prospective employers will compose (or select from a longer list already in their manual) a handful of questions for each of the competencies they have selected. Each one is designed to uncover your experiences in these competencies. These questions will always be phrased in a very specific way, and if you listen carefully, you'll recognize them as behavioral questions easily, because they all really sound the same. They are all asking you to "Tell me a story." Therefore, the questions will all start something like this: "Tell about a time when..."; "When was the last time you..."; "Can you describe a time when..."; or "Describe a situation when...."

3. The third piece of their preparation is to adopt a uniform scoring grid or system for your answers, as the chief goal of behavioral interviewing is to try to turn what has historically been a very subjective process into a more measurable, objective one, and "keeping score" is a good way to do that. (More on this later.)

With this kind of information in hand, most companies will put together a small team of interviewers, usually including one HR person partnered along with two to three others from the department or work team you'd be working in, including your potential boss. Their job is to identify the competencies they want to assess, decide which questions will help them to do that, and select a small team to actually conduct the interviews themselves — typically in a panel-type setting. When you get that first phone call, it will probably be from a member of this group, and they will already be this far along in the process.

What Should You Do To Prepare for Behavior Interviews?

Here's the good news. In the old days, interviews were like pop quizzes, and you never knew what was going to be on them. Behavioral interviews are more like open book tests — you know what's coming, so you are prepared and are very comfortable with the information you need before you walk in the door. Get yourself ready in a couple of ways:

1. You will need to go through your own history of accomplishments, so that you have a list of 'stories' at your disposal that you'll be able to use in the interviews. Use illustrations from internships, classes and school projects, activities, athletic participation, community service, hobbies and work experience as examples of your past behavior. Whether they are personal or professional, be sure to include stories about scoring the winning goal, being elected president of an organization, winning a prize, surfing a big wave, or raising money for charity. Refer back to Module 4 for examples.

2. Review as carefully as possible the job description or posting — or any other printed materials you can lay your hands on — to pick out all the obvious clues as to what the company is looking for in the successful candidate. Almost all job postings have a list of skills or experiences required for the role. Print out a copy, review the list of requirements carefully,

highlighting the ones you can pick out, and make a list of what the employer has identified as important to them.

3. Match up your stories one-by-one to the competencies or skills that are listed in the position description, so that you can chart out which stories of yours fall into the categories or groups of experiences, skills, or credentials that the employer is seeking.

Hint: Because so many companies have adopted a behavioral interviewing program, they are typically very open about and comfortable discussing their interviewing process. They really do want you to understand how to do well in the interview — they have no need to trip you up or cause you to perform poorly. In fact, the opposite is true; they will want to see your "best game." With this information, prior to the interview, you should simply ask the person who calls to schedule the interview for any insight they can provide to help you prepare. You can ask such things as:

- *Should I be prepared specifically for a behavioral interview?*
- *Have you already identified the competencies that you will be assessing for this position? Are you able to share them with me at this time so I can be prepared for the interview?*
- *Are there any additional materials / websites or other information I should study up on before I show up next week?*

The Answers: The Challenge — Action — Result (CAR) Approach to Storytelling

The good news about answering behavioral interview questions is that you only have to learn one format, and then use it over and over again. Every story has three clear and specific sections, or chapters. Following this example, you'll find several templates at the end of the section to help you prepare your own stories in a format similar to this one. Here's how it works:

PART I: CHALLENGE. This is your chance to put the reader inside the story itself, by describing to them the setting or the context of the story — where it took place, who was involved, why it was important, and what your particular involvement or responsibility was. For example:

"Last winter, I took the initiative to apply for grants to pay for a nationally recognized keynote speaker for our awards banquet at the end of the tennis season. As I began the process of researching more options, I learned that this kind of grant is a lot harder to find than I had expected. It turns out that I came up with four different possibilities to raise the money, but each had different application deadlines and requirements for how the money could be used, so I really had to get organized".

PART II: ACTIVITY. This section is your chance to tell the listener what you actually did, or the specific actions you took, one at a time and in sequential order, with a focus on YOUR contribution, even in a team setting. For example:

"Here's how I got organized and moved ahead. First, I used Excel to create a database, with several fields, including grant deadlines, purposes for which the money could be used, the amount of money each grant provided, and the windows of time they could be used. This helped me prioritize and list which grants I could apply for and on what schedule. Next, I reviewed all four grant applications so I could see how each one was similar to the others and different as well. Next I created my own template, and used it to write up the key ideas that needed to be included in the applications, along with the specific plans we had for the funds. Then I incorporated this into one Word file, so I could copy and paste that information into the right field for each application. Then, one after the other, I applied for all four grants, hitting each deadline as required."

PART III: RESULT. This is your chance to show that you actually achieved the results you were looking for, hopefully in a way that you can measure, count, or otherwise quantify. It is also your chance to let the interviewer know what you learned from that accomplishment, to show that you will be able to generate similar results for them when you come on board with the company as their next new hire. The results sections show the interviewer how well the situation played out. For example:

"We were fortunate to find out that the very first grant we applied for did come through, although the group required me to take on additional responsibilities in order to earn the grant money. So I quickly identified a Greek organization who had done some work with a local Boys Club downtown, and they helped us put a new table together for eight

> "Getting a job means you're the product. Refine ten stories for interviews. If you know those stories with intimate detail and tell them over and over again, every behavioral interview question is easy."
>
> —FINANCIAL ADVISOR AND FORMER DIVISION II SOFTBALL PLAYER

underprivileged kids so they could attend the banquet as well. In the end, the event was successful on multiple levels. We hoped to draw about 75 alumnus and other community guests to attend but we got just over 100. We also raised over $10,000 for next year's Florida trip, and finally, we built a whole new fan base for the team from the Boys Club. I really learned a lot from this experience: how to juggle deadlines, to take initiative, and to build new relationships with people who previously didn't know."

The Scoring System

There are a number of different ways that the interview team can assess your performance, and you can miss the larger point of the interview by spending too much time worrying about their scoring system. Have you had experiences in the past that will translate well into this job, and did you get results? While each company or interview committee will vary in their particular system, one of the easiest scoring systems to understand and employ is one that will put you in a good position to prepare for these questions. Think of it this way:

Each of the three components of your Challenge — Action — Result (CAR) answer is worth a maximum of 5 points. For each question, then, there is a 15-point maximum score. Viewing it in this way will ensure that you prepare each of these 3 equally important sections separately and carefully, with your overall goal of creating one unified story.

Additional Thoughts on Behavioral Interviewing

- When you tell a behavioral story, you should assume that the interviewer (or "scorekeeper," if this were an Olympic event) actually wants you to get the maximum number of points, and if they have to, they will help you get them. They will do this by asking follow-up questions that probe for more depth or detail such as, "What made you decide to go that way?" or "How did your team respond to that?" You should both be prepared for, and really welcome, these kinds of questions. They are signs that you are in the hands of a good interviewer who is interested in the story you're telling and is hoping that these questions will pull the last points out of the fire for you before the game is over.

- Your responses need to be specific, detailed, well-rehearsed, and whenever possible, jammed full of numbers (or data or specific information). The more specific your response,

68% of former athletes stated that they did not practice interviewing or engage in a mock interview as an undergraduate.

the more points you'll get. Avoid talking in general or hypothetical terms. The interviewer is not terribly interested in your philosophy or thoughts about the future. Rather, he or she is focused very specifically on the past. You only get to say so many words — make them count.

- There are dozens of lists of sample behavioral questions. Some of these lists have 250 or more sample questions on them. Try not to let this scare you off, or get in the way of your preparation. Of course, no one has 250 stories to tell. Your job is to focus in on the 10-12 stories you can put together that accurately reflect your skills, experiences, and personality. You'll be pleasantly surprised at how far a few solid stories will carry you in this process. The best way to prepare is to focus on what you can bring to an employer — if it matches up, the job will be yours. If not, the employer was looking for someone else the whole time anyway.

- Be sure to be prepared with some "bad" stories, too. Many behavioral questions try to get at how you responded to negative situations. They sound like this: "Tell me about a time that you failed to..."; or "Can you recall an instance when you were unable to forge a good working relationship with..." Of course, we accept the notion that loss, failure, and difficult circumstances make us stronger and more capable, whether as athletes or employees. Be ready to talk honestly about the tough times, but be sure that the story ends with what you learned from that challenge. If you learned it in the past, your next employer doesn't have to worry about teaching you that one in the future. So, maybe a third of your answers should involve your ability to overcome some kind of adversity.

- As we have stressed throughout this book, some of your best stories will certainly come from your athletic endeavors. Yet, you cannot afford to come off as one-dimensional in your job search. You'll have to present yourself to the job market as more than a college athlete. So vary your examples; don't take them all from the playing field.

- In the interview, listen carefully to each question, and pull an example out of your bag of tricks that seems like the best fit for the scenario or question — even if it doesn't feel like a perfect fit. Just tell the story you picked with confidence. Often, the interviewer will be just as focused on the way you answer the question (in terms of CAR) as the content of the question. Provide an appropriate description of how you demonstrated the desired behavior. With practice, you can learn to tailor a relatively small set of examples to respond to a number of diverse behavioral questions.

- If you get called for an interview and they don't ask behavioral questions; you give them behavioral answers anyway. Behavioral interviewing is based on a simple but powerful belief that doesn't change with the way questions are asked. The best predictor of future behavior is still past behavior, whether the company you're meeting with built an interviewing program around it or not. Telling stories that highlight your strengths in the CAR format is your go-to interviewing strategy.

Summary

Behavioral Interviewing is a very specific strategy that is designed in such a way that you are asked questions that will get you to talk about the career-related experiences, behaviors, knowledge, skills, and abilities of your past that the company is focused on, and looking for, in their next new hire. To be fully ready for this strategy, and for any other interview as well, you'll need to:

- Review and flesh out your own accomplishments.
- Turn these accomplishments into "stories" by putting them in a very specific format — the Challenge — Action — Result (CAR) format.
- Carefully read and review the job posting and other information so you can focus your stories on the competencies that the hiring company has decided are important and relevant to the job.

With a good understanding of how companies organize themselves with regard to interviewing strategy, coupled with the right kind and amount of preparation, this is a game you can win.

EXERCISES

RATIONALE: In order to succeed in all job interviews, and specifically in Behavioral Interviews, you'll need to take a look back at some of the previous work you've done in this program, and pull it all together. If you can identify some of the stories from your past that you are particularly proud of, match each of them up with the kinds of skills that employers are looking for, and then tell these stories in a very specific format (Challenge — Action — Result), you can walk into any interview with the confidence that comes from knowing that you are fully prepared.

EXERCISE 12.1: Skill Identification

DIRECTIONS: Refer to an actual job description (the one you used for the exercise in Module 9 or 11 would be ideal) and identify 5 skills, competencies, and qualifications that you think the company is looking for in the ideal candidate, based on that ad. Then write the name of the "story" from your past that demonstrates your capability in that area.

Hint: You should refer back to some of the accomplishments you worked so hard to prepare in Module 4 for this exercise.

Skill #1:

_____

Story:

_____

_____

Skill #2:

_____

Story:

_____

_____

Skill #3:

_____

Story:

_____

_____

Skill #4:

_____

Story:

_____

_____

Skill #5:

_____

Story:

_____

_____

EXERCISE 12.2: **Interview Preparation**

Directions: Write out the response that you would give during an interview to demonstrate your skills and ability in these specific competency areas. Provide your answers to each question using the Challenge — Action — Results (CAR) model. *(Again, you should have done most of this work in Module 5.)*

Skill #1:

_____

CAR Response:

_____

_____

Skill #2:

_____

CAR Response:

_____

_____

Skill #3:

_____

CAR Response:

_____

_____

Skill #4:

_____

CAR Response:

_____

_____

Skill #5:

_____

CAR Response:

_____

_____

MODULE 13
Advanced Resume

I n every sport, the preseason is the time that players focus on sharpening their own skills and bonding with their teammates. But as the first game comes closer, there is a shift in focus, and players and coaches start to emphasize preparation for actual game conditions against their upcoming opponents and other teams in their conference. In much the same way, earlier in this program we introduced the basic concepts of resume design. In this section, we want to get you ready to put that resume, along with cover letters and reference lists, into play in the world of work. Whether you have already put together a first draft, or you are starting from scratch, it's now time to focus on putting your credentials out there in the field. Below are a number of tips, ideas, and suggestions for making your resume the most competitive one possible.

(Tip: If you have not already done so, it will be of significant benefit to you to read or re-read Module 7, Resume Basics, before proceeding.)

The Two Assumptions of Resume Writing

Those of us who have been writing resumes for many years now believe that word processing software was invented just for us, given how much this software has changed the resume design process. Throughout this section, keep the following two assumptions in mind:

1. **THE "WORKHORSE" RESUME:** You should plan to write one solid, all day/every day resume that you will save to your desktop and use regularly. This is the resume that you may use to

post on job boards (when there is not a specific opening) or to put on file in the college career center. When a friend of your mom or dad asks for your resume, they are probably going to get this one. This is the first resume you write, and the one that you will edit and update routinely, for example, when you finish a specific course or training or add a new skill or accomplishment.

2. **ALL YOUR MODIFIED OTHER RESUMES:** The second assumption of resume design is that every resume you ever distribute is likely to be customized, based on what job you are applying for, what organization or industry you are targeting, or who asked for the resume in the first place. You will almost certainly find yourself creating new resumes constantly as you go along, whether they are for different companies, different industries, or different areas of vocational interest, and you may choose to save those as you create them. Yet, by the time you create 2 or 3 or 10 new variations of the resume, you're going to get really confused about what changes you've made to what version under what circumstances. So, when things get murky, you should always plan on going back to that first "workhorse" resume.

Visual/Electronic presentation and preparation

While we know full well that resume management software and computer driven Applicant Tracking Systems (ATS) are prevalent in the job search arena, it is also true that if you do advance to the final stages of any interview process, the odds are very high that you will walk into an interview room to see two to five people all holding a hard copy of your resume in front of them. With this, the visual aesthetics of your resume remain very important. It has been said that most resume screeners scan or skim a resume very quickly (usually within 30 seconds) before making decisions about what or how much to read, so your format should be selected with that in mind.

You will find it easier to manage the resume distribution process if you create a version that is accessible to both ATS and print versions. Most systems today are able to easily manage and file Microsoft Word files, although some experts will recommend that you stay one software version behind the most current upgrade. This ensures that those employers who haven't yet upgraded will still find your resume easy to upload and search. For example, even though the most recent Word document automatic file/format today is .docx, you should stick with saving your resume as a .doc file, just in case your favorite potential employer is still one upgrade (or more!) behind the times.

Additional tips include:

- The tabs and margins should be consistent, and you should avoid using too many different fonts or sizes on your resume.
- Font size should be large enough for the older generation to read, thus we recommend a font size no smaller than 11-point.
- Do not get too fancy with the style of font you use. Use standard fonts such as Verdana, Times New Roman, or Arial.
- Avoid excessive underlining, italics, or other potentially distracting textual elements.
- Avoid boxes and shading on your resume.
- Consider putting either the names of former and current employers, or the job titles you've held — but not both — in bold or in all caps, so that a prospective employer can see, at a glance your most relevant actual work experience.
- As a recent or prospective recent graduate, your resume should be no longer than one page. If you go over one page, be sure to use page numbers.
- It is considered "green" or environmentally sound to print your resume front and back rather than on two separate pages.
- Employ the editing maxim, "every key stroke costs $1," to avoid using unnecessary words and phrases. For example, there is no need to write the word "name," or "references provided upon request." (Of course you will provide them. Why would you feel the need to write that? Were you going to say 'no' if they asked for them?)
- If you need to print hard copies of your resume, they should be printed on good quality white or off-white paper, such as 24# bond, which you can buy at your local office supply store.

Resume Best Practices

LOOK OUT FOR THE MINOR MISTAKES: Misspellings, punctuation errors, and related language mistakes are almost always a knockout punch in the resume screening process. Resume readers assume — and rightfully so — that if you didn't take the time to proofread and perfect your own work in this important process, you're very likely to make the exact same kinds of mistakes when you come to work for them. Of all the reasons for your candidacy to be dismissed from the hiring process, don't let this easy fix be one of them.

41% of former athletes did not have their resumes reviewed as undergraduates.

Ask a friend or family member to review your resume for you. Remove yourself from your resume for some time before giving it a final review. When you stare too long at a resume, you lose sight of important matters and minute details. Writers tend to fall in love with their own writing after a while, so always rely on a second pair of fresh eyes. Be open to feedback, and if you hear the same kinds of criticisms or suggestions from more than one or two sources, it's probably pretty accurate, so pay attention. Remember also that spell check will not always find every misspelled word, and sometimes it does not review words with capital letters or correct spelling of wrong word choices. Many times we forget to review our work carefully, and this could be the difference in getting an interview or not.

A RESUME IS A SALES DOCUMENT: The information on a resume should be presented in a manner that says, "I am a person who has accomplished a great deal. I have been on winning teams, I have met, and often surpassed, others' expectations of me, and I have learned how to do a lot of things, in the workplace, in the classroom, and on the playing field. And, I can bring these skills and attributes to your company. I have achieved great things before, and I can do it again for you." Many resumes don't "sell" simply because the author writes in a voice that reflects a common theme among resume writers: "I was only doing my job," or "I just did what all the other students or teammates did." This mindset causes you to turn what should be a sales and marketing presentation into a simple list of duties and responsibilities set by someone else that you simply checked off as you performed them. Make this resume about you: your skills, your strengths, and your accomplishments. The job search process is, by its very nature, a competition between you and the other applicants, so get your head fully in the game.

47% of former athletes stated that they knew little to nothing about how to effectively write their accomplishments and skills on a resume as undergraduates.

THINK LIKE — AND THEN WRITE TO — THE EMPLOYER: The first draft of any good resume is a love letter to yourself. It's the second draft that sells. That's the one you craft for your next employer, so think like they do. Often, the only thing on the employers' mind is: "Which of these applicants is going to do me the most good, make me the most money, or achieve the largest number of objectives that I set for the position?" Ask yourself, "What would make you that person, the perfect candidate?

What does the employer really want? What special abilities would this person have? What would set a truly exceptional candidate apart?"

If you've done your research on the field and on the job itself, and you've contacted members of your network to see what they can contribute to these questions, you should already have a pretty good idea of the answers. If your resume doesn't address employers' needs, they won't respond to it. Finally, after you feel you have included the information on the resume that really matters, take a close look at what's left. Now you should begin to remove any information that is not actually relevant to the position you are seeking. This way, all the information on the resume feels relevant to your reader, and you can delete the rest that gets in the reader's way. Your key challenge is to identify the skills that an employer wants in the perfect candidate, and focus your resume on how you've developed and used these skills in your own experiences.

WRITING IN THE ACTIVE VOICE & USING PAST TENSE VERBS: Using what your English Composition faculty members refer to as "the active voice" is among the best of tools in the resume writer's toolkit.

Here's how it works: When a sentence in your resume has an action verb in it, the "subject" (in your resume the subject is YOU), performs the action described by the verb. When you are the one who performs, or "acts upon" the verb in such sentences, these sentences are said to be in the "active voice."

English lessons aside, this is why resume writers almost uniformly agree that, whenever possible, you should start each sentence in your resume with a past tense verb (see sample list below). Starting sentences with a past tense verb conveys to the reader directly what you have accomplished over the last several years in the fewest words possible. Remember: verbs show action, so when recruiters review your resume, they learn that you have accomplished specific tasks. This leads them to further assume that you will take similar action again if you are hired for the job — which is exactly the impression you're trying to make. Using an action verb at the beginning of a sentence will increase the strength of your writing, make your writing clearer, and help you make a stronger first impression.

Examples include:

- Designed, developed and distributed customized monthly budget results, providing timely and accurate data for the ticket sales office.

- Recruited and managed a team of 10 volunteers to carry out a campus wide orientation that led to a .25 increase in satisfaction ratings over last year.
- Demonstrated writing skills through the creation of a conference — wide electronic marketing campaign that increased web views by 13%.

Action Verbs

accomplished achieved	demonstrated determined	lectured led
acquired acted	designed developed	made maintained
adapted addressed	devised diagnosed	managed manufactured
adjusted administered	directed dispatched	marketed mediated
advanced advised	distinguished distributed	moderated modified
allocated analyzed	diversified drafted	monitored motivated
applied appraised	edited educated	negotiated observed
approved arranged	eliminated enabled	operated ordered
assembled assigned	encouraged engineered	organized originated
assisted attained	enlisted established	outsold overhauled
audited author	ensured estimated	oversaw participated
automated balanced	evaluated examined	performed persuaded
brought budgeted	executed expanded	planned prepared
built calculated	expedited extracted	presented presided
catalogued chaired	fabricated facilitated	prioritized processed
changed clarified	familiarized fashioned	produced programmed
coached collected	finalized focused	projected promoted
communicated compared	forecast formulated	proposed provided
compiled completed	founded gathered	publicized published
composed computed	generated graded	purchased recommended
computerized conceptualized	guided handled	reconciled recorded
conceived concluded	headed up identified	recruited reduced
conducted conserved	illustrated implemented	referred regulated
consolidated contained	improved increased	rehabilitated related
continued contracted	indoctrinated influenced	remodeled repaired
contributed controlled	informed initiated	reported represented
coordinated corrected	innovated inspected	researched restored
corresponded counseled	instructed insured	restructured retrieved
created critiqued	integrated interpreted	reversed reviewed
cut decreased	interviewed introduced	revised revitalized
delegated decided	invented investigated	saved scheduled
defined delivered	kept launched	schooled screened

selected serviced	stimulated streamlined	translated traveled
set shaped	strengthened suggested	trimmed updated
screened selected	summarized supervised	upgraded validated
simplified skilled	surveyed systemized	worked wrote
sold solidified	tabulated taught	
solved specified	tested trained	

MORE THAN EVER, FOCUS ON ACHIEVEMENT-DRIVEN AND QUANTIFIABLE RESULTS. As we have noted frequently in earlier sections of this text, it is critical to the resume design process that you explain not just what you did, but also how well you did it, and how your efforts helped the team, customer, or organization. Remember, whether these accomplishments are individual achievements, things you did as part of a team, or the result of your leadership of others, they are the best evidence that you are the person who should be hired into a role where you can use these skills over and over again. People reading resumes like numbers, so work at uncovering and listing the number of people on the teams you have led or been a member of, the amount of money your event may have raised, the profits generated from your project, or the grades you received for your efforts.

DESCRIBE CLEARLY ANY ACTIVITIES THAT EMPLOYERS MAY NOT BE FAMILIAR WITH. Because you've been on campus for a few years, you may have developed a vocabulary or a list of abbreviations that you have used for so long that you have come to believe that everyone understands. Fundraisers, Greek events, athletics, and campus organizations sometimes require a bit of explanation to those who have been away from school for a while. Define acronyms and abbreviations.

CONSIDER A TECHNICAL SKILLS SECTION. This is primarily for those of you with highly technical skills or training, including engineering, computer programming, or health sciences, for example. This section might include hardware or software applications, expertise on specific laboratory equipment, specific credentials or certifications, sections of qualifying exams already passed, or other technical information. If such training and expertise is critical to your marketability, consider placing this section immediately below the Summary section and above your Work Experience. If you are targeting a non-technical position, on the other hand, this section is optional. If you do include it, it would most likely be placed near or at the bottom of the resume.

TAKE A HARD LOOK AT THE BOTTOM PORTION OF THE RESUME. There is a tendency on the part of some recent graduates to place too much emphasis on this section, while others will waste the opportunity to show their leadership and other accomplishments fully while on campus. As you review this section, think about the following:

- For any awards you received that were based on academic performance, you can place these under the Education section, and indicate clearly what the award was for. If you have received awards or significant recognition from non-academic sources, you may choose to highlight these in a separate section, entitled "Awards and Recognition." If you authored or co-authored research papers, research findings, or articles that were published in professional/academic journals or you presented at an academic conference, be sure to list these here as well.
- Include any significant leadership roles you've held, particularly if your membership in an association or volunteer activities with a local group would enhance your appeal as a prospective employee. This section can be titled "Civic/Community Leadership" or "Professional and Community Memberships."

> *"My biggest regret is not having enough career-related experience during my undergraduate career. It really put me at a disadvantage when I was trying to write an effective resume. I didn't have enough work-related accomplishments that I could highlight."*
> —CUSTOMER SERVICE REPRESENTATIVE AND FORMER DIVISION II WOMEN'S SWIMMER

WHAT ABOUT THE "PERSONAL INTERESTS" SECTION? Most resume writers will advise you against such a section. Yet, under the right circumstances, this kind of information can really underscore your knowledge of a specific subject related to your vocational goals. Additionally, this section allows you, in just a few words, to create some common ground or spark an ice-breaking conversation in the interview. In most cases, your personal interests will be irrelevant to the job you're seeking, and so, when in doubt, you should refer back to the "every keystroke costs $1" theory — and leave it out.

The most important thing to remember is this: You are writing to a potential employer, and it's your job to figure out what they have decided are the most important skills, experiences, and traits for their next new hire to have. Then, you write or edit your resume to sell them on the fact that you are that person!

Sample Resume:

MARGARET ANN

(504) 785-5555   MARGARET.ANN@GMAIL.COM

Customer Service / Sales Support / Marketing / Promotions / Project Management

2015 graduate in Sport Administration with experience gained from multiple internships and volunteer opportunities. Leadership, communication, and management skills gained from volunteer coaching. Excellent work ethic, keen ability to interact with others, and deliver on commitments made.

PROFESSIONAL EXPERIENCE

HEAVRIN UNIVERSITY — Louisville, KY   **Spring 2015**
Private, historic four year University that provides an outstanding education environment in an intimate setting to students.

Director of Operations (Intern)

Reported directly to the Head Soccer Coach. Provided a range of administrative and project management support. Created and managed an Excel database utilized for recruiting, parent and alumni relations. Managed all aspects of a key community outreach event for the department.

- **Event Planning / Project Management:** Collaborated with Special Olympics of Kentucky to organize a community outreach soccer clinic hosted by the Spalding Women's Soccer team. Customized the soccer training session to help participants build soccer skills and self -esteem. Developed press releases and authored an article / blog, utilizing social and traditional media strategies to promote the event.
- **Marketing / Communications:** Developed newsletters and emails to communicate with parents of student — athletes. Created a system in Microsoft Outlook to easily correspond and maintain relationships with recruits.

UNIVERSITY OF LOUISVILLE ATHLETIC DEPARTMENT — Louisville, KY   **Fall 2014**
One of the nation's leading athletic departments with a national reputation for preparing student athletes for leadership and educational achievements through athletic competition.

Ticket Office (Intern)

Provided direct customer service and back office sales support for walk up and other ticket sales strategies. Processed account payments and performed a range of related account management activities. Worked with Marketing team on promotional campaigns to increase revenue via season ticket holders and other potential ticket buyers locally and regionally.

- **Customer Service:** Worked with ticket office department to maximize ticket sales through season tickets, walk up sales, and promotional packages. Processed payments for account holder donations.

- **Project Management:** Developed an alternative handicap ticket sales governance policy to guide and monitor ticket allocations for athletic events. Reviewed best practices in place with other sport organizations nationally.

UNITED 1996 F.C.   **2014-2015**
Soccer Coach
Organized and ran practices for team. Maintained communications with coaches and parents.

EDUCATION / COMMUNITY SERVICE

B.S., Sport Administration — University of Louisville — Louisville, KY   **Spring 2015**
- **Dean's List:** Spring 2014-2015
- **Volunteer Soccer Coach:** Fall 2014
- **Soccer Coaching USSF E License,** 2014
- **Volunteer Jam Active Tap N Run and Republic Bank Big Hit ½ Marathon**

Cover Letters

Many experts in job search strategy today are split on the current value and use of cover letters. Here, in a nutshell, is the current debate:

1. "No one" ever reads cover letters anymore, since resumes are screened by a computer, using an Applicant Tracking System (ATS).

vs.

2. Okay, it's true that most ATS don't "read" cover letters, but in fact some systems do allow you to cut and paste such correspondence into a separate dialogue box, and that information may very well find its way to an interviewing team. Even if every cover letter written doesn't get read, you have no excuse not to write them. If it DOES get read and that information finds its way to the hiring team in just one case, and you get hired, was it worth it?

Our opinion is absolutely the latter one. While we certainly understand the merits of the first point above, that not every cover letter will get read these days, we also firmly believe that — if it does in fact get read — it provides you with just the kind of competitive advantage you always want. It gives you an extra chance to sell your candidacy to the hiring team. Your cover letter and supporting materials may not be read entirely until later in the process when they have narrowed the search group to just a few finalist, so make sure your work is perfect.

So, whether you copy and paste a cover letter into a separate dialogue box on an online application system, or you email a cover letter with your resume in response to a job posting, we think that you should take advantage of every opportunity that you can to communicate your skills to the employer.

Specific suggestions for cover letter composition and design include:

- Address the cover letter by name to the most important person in the hiring process you can uncover at the company, whether that is the key recruiter or the hiring manager. Conversely, never use "To whom it may concern" or "Dear sir or madam." If you can't find a name, then, in the place of the "Dear _____" section, use the job title instead ("Re: your open Human Resources Assistant position").

  Hint: If a name is not included in the posting, try simply picking up the phone and asking the employer if you can have the name of the hiring manager — even that small amount of research may put you in a positive light against the people who didn't bother to try to make this personal connection to the employer.

- Always indicate the name of the position you are applying for, and how you learned about the opening, whether in the salutation or in the first paragraph. When possible, be sure to include personal referrals here as well, (*i.e.*, "My coach and mentor, William Bryant, let me know that you are seeking a...").
- Tailor the letter to the specific organization and the responsibilities of the position. A generic cover letter lacks interest to a potential employer. Include three or four very specific reasons why you line up perfectly with the specifications of the job or the employer. Highlight these with bullet points or other formatting tricks in the body of the letter, so these experiences or accomplishments jump off the page for the reader.
- Do not exceed one page. If you are mailing the cover letter using snail mail, use the same matching high quality paper that you're using for your resume. Don't hand write your letter, and don't let any grammatical, punctuation, or spelling errors slip through.

- Close the cover letter with a request for a face-to-face interview. Always thank the employer for his/her consideration and offer to follow up with them if you have not heard from them soon.

Cover Letter Example:

Dear Mr. Collins:

I am writing in response to the advertisement for an Engineering Analyst found on your website dated March 15, 2017.

I am a recent graduate of Purdue University with a Bachelor's Degree in Electrical Engineering. Most recently, as a second semester intern for Collins Manufacturing — a division of Steel Industries — I enjoyed significant exposure to that company's Engineering, Technical, EH&S, and Quality organizations.

My background includes numerous examples of serving in leadership roles, both on campus and in work, internship, and athletic settings. My experience includes:

- Using Excel spreadsheets, including pivot tables, to assist manufacturing team leaders in the preparation of budgets and strategic business plans for Collins.
- Rotating through internship assignments in Lean manufacturing, reengineering and restructuring operations to learn every aspect of the manufacturing and distribution process.
- Shadowing an implementation team that used ISO and TQM principles to foster teamwork and continuous improvement.
- Serving as Chief Fundraiser for our volunteer organization on campus, Athletes for Alumni, where I led my team of 25+ college athletes to establish effective relationships with prior graduates of Purdue, and raised $15,000 in donations from our alumni for our non -profit charitable organization.

I would be happy to provide you with further information to assist in your review of my credentials. If I have not heard from you in 10-14 days, I hope you won't mind if I follow up with a phone call to assure that you have all the information you need.

Sincerely,
Katherine Smith

References

In most hiring situations, the very last step in the process comes to a head when your next employer asks you to provide a list of references (typically three or four) who can verify the wonderful things you've said about yourself over the course of the interview process. Since this is usually the last step in the process, many job seekers put off preparing this list (or speaking with those who will be on the list). You can easily make missteps when the time comes, if you are not prepared and provide a list of people who are not ready to support you.

You should certainly begin now preparing a list of such people. Put together a preliminary list of 6 to 10 people who might be willing to serve in this capacity. If you're lucky, almost all of them will agree to do this for you, and when the time comes, you'll be able to select and match up 3 to 4 of them who can best promote you, depending on the circumstances, the nature of the job, or the specific employer. As you prepare your list of references, here are a few tips to keep in mind:

- Think carefully about who is best suited to be a reference for you. You'll want nothing less than a 100 percent approval rating from these folks. Before you start to fill in some of the categories of references (see below), make sure that your entire list of references will say absolutely wonderful things about you, all day and every day. No exceptions to this rule.

- You should select a few different categories of references. For those with significant experience in actual paying jobs on or off campus, select a few references who are previous supervisors and co-workers. You should also consider including educational mentors, coaches, others from your athletic endeavors, references from internships or volunteer work, academic advisors, and professors. Think also about people who have worked with you as peers, co-workers, or teammates, as often your next employer will want this type of insight into your ability to get along with others.

- Get permission to use someone as a reference first. Before you list someone as a reference, you'll need to ask whether the person would be comfortable in that capacity. Importantly, be prepared for some to decline your request — for whatever reason. Recognize this as a good thing — better now than if/when a potential employer called and they gave you a less than stellar review! Give them each an easy way out, just in case. You might want to make your request via email, for example. Then, if you don't hear back, you have your answer.

- Get all the contact details you can for each reference, making sure to get complete information: full name, current title, company name, business address, and contact information (daytime phone, email, cell phone, etc.). Put your references into categories, such as employer, academic, and personal, and include a notation regarding their relationship to you on your reference sheet, for example, former coach, professor, teammate, mentor, etc.

- Coach your references *before* they get reference calls. Make sure they always have a copy of your most current resume, know your key accomplishments and skills, and are aware of the calls they might get and from whom. Most importantly, make sure that they will be available to the reference checkers at the right time. Remember, you want to make it as easy as possible for the employer to find your references. If this is the last step in the hiring process, you want to make sure your potential employer can connect with your reference so they can make you a job offer. Some employers will not extend a job offer until all references have been checked.

Sample Reference List:

References

Terry Dunigan
Director, Human Resources
National Containers Corporation
5130 Ontario Lakes Pkwy
Mishawaka, IN 46545
812-555-3210
tduniganh@ncc.net
Relationship: Supervisor of senior year internship

Joe O'Keeffe

Vice President, Marketing

Jones Legal Services

1212 N. Riley Street

Chicago, IL 60610

312-555-3930

jokeeffe@jls.net

Relationship: Supervisor of junior year internship

Chris Warren

NCAA Tournament Site Manager

77 Dexter Pkwy

Westwood, KS 66205

620-555-0077

cwarren@aol.com

Relationship: Mentor

Michael Tarver

Swimming Coach

DePaul University Athletics

Chicago, IL 60602

312-555-1616

mtarver@depaul.net

Relationship: Varsity swim coach

Summary

At this point, the actual execution of your job search might be right around the corner. Like many projects, having the right tools in your toolbox can make any task a whole lot easier to pull off. In the case of a solid job search strategy, you'll need:

YOUR FIRST SOLID RESUME: Although you will find it necessary to make edits or changes to your resume based on the type of job you are applying for, you'll need to have that first solid workhorse resume with the basics included.

Secondly, you'll need a good template or starting point for the **COVER LETTERS** that will accompany many of your applications. Knowing the format and style you'll use, and saving these on your desktop and in the cloud, will make the inevitable process of tailoring cover letters for your prospective audiences later all the easier.

Finally, you'll need a list of well-prepared **REFERENCES** who are ready and willing to help. These key members of your job search team will need to be updated before you distribute their names, of course, and some will be more appropriate to call on than others, depending on circumstances, but having that preliminary list of references on call is a solid start.

With these key materials in place ahead of time, you'll be much more prepared to kick off the job search process when the time comes.

Career Spotlight

OLIVIA (LONEY) BOYER is currently a Business Intelligence Analyst at Cerner Corporation. She graduated from the University of Kansas with a Bachelor's of Science degree in Accounting, and was an oarswomen on the rowing team. Olivia is continuing her education through taking night classes to obtain her Master's of Accounting.

EXERCISES

RATIONALE: With the proliferation of automated/electronic resume processing systems in place today, many people are skipping the whole cover letter process, which makes us believe all the more strongly that you can create a huge competitive advantage for yourself by going the extra step to craft a cover letter that lets employers know — beyond the resume — how you can help them solve the problems you know from your research that they are experiencing. Still, it is a time-consuming effort, so we'll help make it easier.

EXERCISE 13.1: Cover Letter

DIRECTIONS: Pull up from your earlier work in this program — or fresh off your favorite job board — a job posting/advertised position that is of interest to you. Go through the ad carefully and use the information that you gather from a variety of sources to fill in the template below. **(Note: Be sure to refer to the sample cover letter in this section to further flesh out the content.)**

Name

_____

Address

_____

Address (look for both URL/Web address and physical)

_____

Dear _____:
(can you find a name? No "to whom it may concern" allowed).

Given my interest in _____, I was excited to find your advertisement on _____ dated _____ for a with _____. I am very excited about being considered for this position, and my resume is enclosed for your review.

I hope that my resume will cover most of the information you will need to evaluate my skills and accomplishments. Yet, I wanted to point out a few specific aspects of my background in this letter, which I hope will be helpful to you as you consider my application:

- Add 3-4 bullet points here that really focus on the specific job as a result of your research

- _____

- _____

- _____

I am confident that I would be able to help you in additional ways as well, and that I would be a strong member of your team. I would enjoy discussing this opportunity in person. Please call me at _____ or email me at _____ to set up a meeting. Thank you for your time, and I look forward to hearing from you.

Sincerely,
Your Name_____

Enclosure: Resume

RATIONALE: Typically, the very last step in the hiring process will be a check of your references. When you get this far, it's pretty close to being your game to lose — but you can still lose it. Your list needs to be well thought out, and your references should be ready for the call to come and easy to reach.

EXERCISE 13.2: **Reference List**

DIRECTIONS: Using the template found earlier in this module, create your own reference list as if you were asked to provide them today. Be sure that you can track down and include all the information listed in the sample found earlier in this module for guidance.

Reference #1

Name:

_____

Title:

_____

Organization:

_____

Address:

_____

Email:

_____

Phone Number:

_____

Relationship:

_____

Reference #2

Name:

_____

Title:

_____

Organization:

_____

Address:

_____

Email:

_____

Phone Number:

_____

Relationship:

_____

Reference #3

Name:

_____

Title:

_____

Organization:

_____

Address:

_____

Email:

_____

Phone Number:

_____

Relationship:

_____

Reference #4

Name:

_____

Title:

_____

Organization:

_____

Address:

_____

Email:

_____

Phone Number:

_____

Relationship:

_____

Reference #5

Name:

_____

Title:

_____

Organization:

_____

Address:

_____

Email:

_____

Phone Number:

_____

Relationship:

_____

MODULE 14

Evaluating and Negotiating a Job Offer

Have you ever heard someone ask, what would happen if that car-chasing neighborhood dog ever actually caught the car? It's an old expression used to describe the feeling of confusion people sometimes have when they finally reach a long sought after goal, and then don't know what to do next. Similarly, the day will come when you will actually receive that first job offer, and you too may not know exactly what to do with it. After all this hard work, you're going to find it very tempting to jump right up and accept that offer on the spot. Yet, this last decision in the rigorous job search process can have a significant impact on you, your family, your career trajectory, and so many other things. It's critical that you take a step back to assess — and perhaps talk further with your potential employer about — whether this is the job that is truly the right one for you.

Before you accept a job offer too quickly, you'll want to take some time to fully understand the offer, considering how it fits with your personality, expectations, and long term career plans. Fit is the most important concept to understand when looking for a job. You want to make sure the job is a fit for the employer, fit for you, and fit for your career goals. You will want to review and clarify all the details of the offer, and identify any aspects of the contract that will require further attention or discussion before you can make a good decision. In this module, you will learn how to acknowledge, evaluate, negotiate and accept/reject a job offer.

Getting the Offer

When that telephone rings, you pick it up, and you hear the voice of a recruiter or hiring manager on the other end calling to let you know that they'd like you to come to work for them, you're going to be excited, nervous, and surprised — and you're probably going to act like it. And that is a good thing. Yet, to effectively manage this conversation you should:

1. **EXPRESS DELIGHT, ENTHUSIASM, and EXCITEMENT** at the news that you have been selected. Whatever happens down the line, you want the person on the other end to hear clearly that you are interested and really want the job. This tone, when set early, will make all the potential discussions down the road easier for all involved, as you will be communicating from the beginning that you really do want to work there, and that you're absolutely sure that, as soon as you have the offer in writing and can review it in its entirety, you will soon be talking to them about start date and getting scheduled in for new hire orientation. That's the way every hiring manager wants to feel in these circumstances, and the alternative, which feels like you're playing "hard to get" or "standoffish," serves no good purpose in these kinds of circumstances. When this call comes, it is your job to set a tone of excitement and collaboration from the outset.

2. **CLARIFY THE NEXT STEPS IN THE PROCESS:** The recruiter may begin at this point to list various components of the offer: starting salary, weeks of vacation, health insurance benefits, etc. This is a natural part of the process, and you should listen carefully and take a few notes along the way. BUT, while maintaining that cheerful and optimistic tone, do not agree to or commit to any part or piece of the offer at this time. Your goal at this point is very clear, you want to receive the offer in writing. You should communicate this directly to the hiring manger. You want to obtain the entire offer — in all its glorious and often mundane detail — in writing, so you can sit at your kitchen table and review the offer. While you are waiting to receive the offer in writing, you do NOT want to waste any of your leverage by being drawn into a "negotiation" in this initial call. This call is way too early to begin negotiating because you do not have all of the facts of the offer. Instead, you want to have the chance to list and compare all the components of the offer before making this important decision. If the hiring manager presses you to respond to the proposed salary, for example, you should answer happily and enthusiastically that you are delighted to have an offer to evaluate, but — if it's okay with them — could you please have the time to take a look at the whole thing before you respond to any specific piece, including the starting salary of the offer? The point here is that everything in the offer will have some degree of value to

you — financial, personal, professional, or otherwise, and inevitably, some will hold more value to you than others. You would be foolish to respond to the wrong one at the wrong time in the wrong way, before you've done your due diligence, and they know this too. So, just express your excitement about receiving and studying the offer, in its entirety.

3. Before you hang up, ask when would be a **GOOD TIME TO FOLLOW-UP TO DISCUSS THE NEXT STEPS** in the process. That is very different language than asking, "How long will I have to accept or reject" the offer, or, "When do you need an answer?" Even though that is the purpose of your statement, it sets the stage for the "discussion" (never a "negotiation") to come. Yet, the employer will have a timeline in mind, and it is important that you know theirs — and yours — for the next steps in the process. You can reasonably expect that you'll be given at least 24-48 hours to review the offer after you receive it in writing. If the employer doesn't provide a timeframe, you should feel comfortable asking for at least this amount of time to review the offer. In any case, you should not feel pushed into an acceptance on the spot, as that's not a good idea for you, and employers should not reasonably expect you to respond that quickly. Even if they do ask for an immediate response, you should still ask for at least 24 hours to evaluate the written offer and do your due diligence.

Reviewing and Evaluating the Offer

As mentioned above, the first step after getting the offer is to get the entire offer in writing. If this is your first shot at a "real" job, then you've got a whole new lesson in front of you; there is an almost dizzying number of possible pieces and parts to a job offer. While you should not be expected to understand every nuance of a job offer at this early juncture in your career, it is important to begin to distinguish between two different kinds of conversations you may have with the hiring company — those things you simply don't understand (what the heck is a "stock option five-year cliff vest schedule"?), as opposed to the issues you do understand, but want to potentially discuss/ negotiate/push back on before making a final decision.

But, first things first. Remember those wonderful assessment instruments you took and reviewed early on? Now is the time to see how this offer stacks up against your MBTI type, your top themes on the SII, and the "must-haves" on your Values assessment exercise. Think back through the criteria you established when you first got started with this career management exploration, as you were just beginning to target certain companies, organizations, industries, and jobs. How does this offer stack up from a personality and cultural fit standpoint? As laborious as all those exercises were that you went through before, you can begin to see how important these issues are to your overall career plans. It may be that this review will raise some important questions about your fit with the company or the job before you come to a final decision. In any case, remember to look inside yourself first and remind yourself of what you truly value and need from a job. Then, you can review the offer again with this in mind.

Next, let's take a look at a checklist of items that may be included in your job offer. Here are a few basics of a job offer that you will want to review prior to making your final decision:

- **SALARY:** For many of us, this is the single most important issue to evaluate. Yet, as you look at the offer in its entirety, you may discover that, in some cases, the salary may only represent around two-thirds of the financial value of the entire compensation package. Be careful not to get too hung up on the salary figure until you've identified the value of the rest of the offer. There are lots of ways to ask for more money down the line, but before you make plans to do that, evaluate the salary carefully against both your own financial needs and against the salary survey/research you've done up to this point. If, for example, you want more money than was offered, but the offer is a fair and reasonable one based on market information, you're going to have a harder time moving the employer on this issue. Therefore, it will be all the more important to see where else within the offer there may be some wiggle room you can both agree on. This is also why it is important to have an understanding of the market value of jobs prior to applying.

- **ADDITIONAL SOURCES OF INCOME:** You'll want to clarify whether there is a bonus plan, and, if so, what has to happen in order for it to be paid out, and when does it get paid out. Most often, bonuses are calculated based on some combination of the employer's overall financial performance plus the employee's individual performance, and it will be helpful for you to evaluate as specifically as you can just how that formula works. You may also ask whether bonuses have been paid over the last 3–5 years, as this is as good indicator of the likelihood that you will receive a bonus in the upcoming years. In other cases, you may be offered a commission structure, with your income based in part — or even totally — on your sales results. Also, ask if the company offers a profit-sharing program, and, if so, what the eligibility requirements would be for your participation.

- **THE OVERALL BENEFITS PACKAGE:** This is the area in which the company spends a lot of their time and money, and some of these "perks" or benefits are often hard to fully understand. Be sure that the company provides you with a written summary of its benefits plan. As you evaluate the benefits package, pay attention to:

  ▷ *Health Insurance:* Employers today offer a wider array of health insurance offerings than ever, due at least in part to the complexities associated with newer legislation that affects the entire health insurance marketplace. You may be offered various degrees of financial support or company sponsored coverage for health, dental, and/or vision coverage, as well as both short and long-term disability. This disability coverage provides you with an income if you are unable to work for an extended period of time due to poor health or other reasons. These policies vary a great deal, and may provide coverage just for you (the employee), or it may extend to your family members as well. In most cases, your employer will make some financial contribution to the cost of this coverage, and you will be expected to pay the rest, in the form of a deduction form your paycheck. These costs to you can vary widely, and could make the difference between a "good" and a "bad" offer, so evaluate these issues carefully. If you don't understand them fully, ask to meet with a member of the Human Resources team for further explanation before accepting or declining the offer.

  ▷ *Vacations, Holidays, Sick Days, and Paid Time Off:* Paid Time Off (PTO) policies also continue to evolve to match today's evolving job market. Many companies now combine two formerly separate categories of paid time off — vacation pay and sick pay — into one aggregated number of days awarded to the employee. For example, what might previously have been an offer of two weeks paid "vacation" and another one week of paid "sick time" might now be offered to you as a full three weeks of paid time off (PTO). In such cases, you'll be compensated at your regular rate of pay for 15 days away from work, whether you're sick, or whether you're on the beach somewhere. Also, paid time off may not be immediately available to you; instead, you may need to be on the payroll for a few months before you can take time off, so you'll want to get in one last vacation before your first day of work. You should also clarify if you can carry over unused paid time off from one year to the next. Some companies will let you carry a few paid days over into the next year, while others may pay you for them. Some companies have a PTO rule that you cannot carry over any unused days to the following year, so you'll want to have these policies clarified as a part of your due diligence process.

▷ *Performance and Salary Review Process:* Be sure to ask about policies that govern the performance review process, as these discussions and processes will have a direct impact on any salary increases that you will be able to earn. It is important to know how your performance will be evaluated by your superiors from the outset, of course, so that you can plan to make an immediate and positive impression on your employer. The timing of the performance review process is also important, as it will likely govern when you will first be eligible for a salary increase. Some companies, for example have a policy to evaluate you one year from date of hire, but others will complete all employees' reviews by one uniform date (i.e., they may conduct all performance reviews by December 31), so this schedule will dictate when your first chance at a raise. Depending on their schedule, you may even find yourself asking for an early performance review, so that you won't be penalized from a salary standpoint by the schedule. Finally, you should try to determine the organization's record with regard to salary increases as a result of these reviews. For example, if the company historically only gives very small raises every year, you'd want to be sure to save your negotiating topics for those that might be more financially rewarding, like bonus structures, or even negotiate for more PTO.

▷ *Travel Reimbursement:* If the job requires travel, be sure to clarify the policy regarding reimbursable expenses. You may be provided with a company — issued credit card; some companies, on the other hand, ask you to pay all expenses out of your own pocket, and then get reimbursed by the employer. In a lesser number of cases, you might be responsible for your own expenses — but you'll be eligible to deduct all those expenses on you income taxes at the end of the year. This sounds complicated, but your employer should be able to provide you with very specific information and help on these issues — if you seek it out.

▷ *Retirement:* Be sure to learn whether the organization offers an opportunity for you to save for your retirement, and — if so — how it is structured. Often you will be asked to contribute to your own retirement — in the form of pre — tax payroll deductions, and often they'll then match your contribution up to a certain point. For example, if you choose to have 6% of your salary deducted from your paycheck to be invested for your retirement, then your employer will contribute another 3%; this is called the "employer match." In some cases, you have to remain with the company for a prescribed period of time in order to keep the money they put into your account — but you always get to keep the amount you contributed personally.

Hint: This is one of the great perks of retirement plans/benefit packages, as it is essentially free money. You should definitely start saving for your retirement from the beginning of your career, so when an employer agrees to match your investment, this is a great deal. Remember, the earlier you start contributing to your retirement the sweeter the rewards and the more money you will have when you retire.

> ▷ ***Working arrangements:*** Get as much information as possible on the company's position on how — and where — you will be expected to work. You may be expected to show up at the office every day at 8:30am, and at your desk or cube from morning until quitting time, while others have policies that allow for a range of flexible scheduling alternatives, including working from home for some or part of the day.

- **FINAL THOUGHTS TO CONSIDER:** Ask whether the employer pays for parking or commuting expenses. If you will be relocating for the job, they may also have funds set aside to help you offset some of the relocation costs. Whether you anticipate becoming a new father or mother in the years to come, you should also ask about the company's maternity or paternity leave policy.

- **SIGN-ON BONUSES:** In some industries (mostly business related) when an employer and an employee find themselves very close to a deal, and with only a few small and even unrelated issues still at stake, the company will authorize a one-time signing bonus, payable to you right after you join the company, to cover some percentage, if not all, of those remaining outstanding issues.

After reviewing all of this information from top to bottom, you should make two separate lists:

1. The first list contains the items in the offer that you simply don't understand and need clarification on. Almost every candidate for a position with a new employer will have a

short list of these, and it is important to distinguish these from the items found on your second list.

2. The second list contains the two to three things you would like to bring up with the organization in hopes that the employer will have some flexibility on these. You should try to list them in their order of importance to you (from most important to least important) while at the same time always keeping in mind the immortal words of Mick Jagger:

> *"You can't always get what you want; but if you try sometime you just might find you get what you need."*
> —Mick Jagger

3. With this in mind, review both lists. Write down what you simply don't know, and if there are any "walk away" point(s) in the offer. These are issues that, if not resolved, would result in you having to reject the offer, no matter what. As you prepare for your conversation with the potential employer, ask yourself this truly important question: "If, after your next conversation with the company, nothing in this offer is changed, would you still take the job?" This is the best way to know for yourself if you have such concerns, and, if so, which are the ones that matter the most.

Discussing (not "Negotiating") the Offer

All right, let's get this out of the way early: The word "negotiate" is a troublesome one in the world of job search, and we would all be better served by getting rid of it altogether. In fact, it is a perfectly good word when interpreted correctly, as it is intended to define a successful collaboration, an event or occasion in which people work together to reach a common goal. "Negotiations" are typically seen as adversarial relationships, where someone wins while another loses; one gives while the other gets. Frankly, even using the word in the context of evaluating and discussing job offers has gotten more than one job seeker in trouble, and for no good reason. We recommend the word — and the actual practice — of "discussion" rather than "negotiation." We encourage you to remember that by the time an employer extends you a job offer, they have decided that they really want to hire you. The organization likes you. Its leaders think you'll fit in. They have looked closely at several other candidates for this job, and they've decided they want to hire you. This means that, at this point in the process, they will do whatever they can to help you join the team. IF THEY CAN. In short, they are not your opponent; they are your (potential) teammate. Assume that they are ready to get this hiring process over with for good, and just want to get back to work, hopefully with you.

So, your job will be to let them know what you have considered and thought about as you have evaluated their offer and to ask if they can help you with the concerns that might have come up as you reviewed the offer. Picture yourself pulling your chair around to the same side of the table as theirs — not opposing each other from two different sides. They won't give you what they can't, or what they don't have to give. That's how you should approach the next step in the process: as a "discussion," not a "negotiation."

Making the Call

With the discussion in mind, you should simply plan to call the person who made you the offer, with your two lists in hand. In that call, share with them openly that you have two lists. Be sure to frame the content of both lists as a series of questions, not demands. Work though the list of issues that you do not understand first, as the answers to these questions may have an impact (positively or negatively) on the potentially more difficult discussion of your second list.

Next, lay out your remaining concerns from your second list, briefly, in order, so that your **partner** can tell how close to a deal (or how far apart) you are, from the outset. Don't be too quick to offer solutions to your concerns, as that is their job. For example, you can say, "Do you have any flexibility at all with regard to the starting salary?" However, you may want to wait before answering your own question by saying something like, "I was thinking I sure would like another $5,000 a year."

For each item you bring up, be prepared to discuss your reasons for doing so. For example, if you plan to inquire about a higher salary, you'll need first to think about what additional skills you offer that would justify this increase over their initial offer, or be ready to share the results of a salary survey you uncovered that shows others commanding a higher salary than their offer for the same kind of work. This kind of upfront work is particularity helpful when the person you're talking with doesn't have the authority to make the final decision. In this way, you're giving that person the information he or she need in order to represent your concerns effectively to the decision-maker.

As this discussion develops, keep track of the progress made on your original checklist. As the conversation winds up, either of you may find it necessary to schedule a final wrap up call or email to finalize "the deal," especially if the recruiter or contact person has to go back to get permission to offer some of the points you initially agree to together. Close with an enthusiastic desire to hear what the employer will come back with, continuing to let the organization know that you hope to be working together soon. Be sure to thank the person for his or her help in listening to and agreeing to answer your concerns. Finally, keep in mind these few things:

- Sometimes the first offer is the best they have to give, and sometimes it isn't. You're never going to know this, but don't make either assumption.
- Some will tell you that, after you receive an offer, responding with anything at all other than "yes" can jeopardize the offer. This is a true statement, but you can also counteract it with the right tone and approach. If you approach the conversation openly and sincerely, then typically, the worst case scenario is that they will simply say "no, the offer will remain as is," and then they'll wait for your final decision.
- Remember that employers want to meet your needs if they can, but sometimes they simply don't know what your needs are. Or they can sometimes simply forget, even with the best of intentions, to tell you about a certain benefit, even though it's standard policy. In short, assume positive intent on the employer's behalf, until you learn anything to the contrary. You might find yourself pleasantly surprised at how accommodating they become once you voice your concerns.
- In almost all cases, they want you to take the job, and they want you to be happy. Really!

Declining a Job Offer

In most cases, the back and forth discussions that will take you from that initial job offer to the final version will go fairly quickly, and soon enough, you'll be ready to make your final decision. If, after all your deliberations, you come to the conclusion that this is not the right job for you, you'll need to turn the offer down in a professional manner, without burning any bridges along the way.

Hint: Here's the simplest reason to turn down an offer respectfully and diplomatically. Because the company recognized your talent and your fit with the organization, and in the near future a more suitable role may open up at the company. Many successful job seekers have gotten a second offer that came from a coveted employer that was better than the first. This is what you're shooting for: When that next job at the same company comes along, you get an early phone call, and you cut right to the front of the line on this interview/search process — and then land the kind of offer you had hoped for last time out!

Although circumstances may cause a different course, you should plan on giving your response as soon as you've made your decision. You should respond initially by phone rather than email or letter. You'll want to strike a balance when offering your reason for turning them down between being honest and forthright without seeming to blame the organization for your decision. Your reasons should be more about you — your values, goals, or aspirations — than about their crummy pay scale, weak bonus plan, or uncomfortable cubical. Take the high road and always look for a way to leave the situation without regrets, remember you do not get another chance to redo a difficult conversation or awkward moment.

Then, follow up with a brief written note or email that covers the same ground. It doesn't have to be long or overly apologetic. Try something like this:

Dear Ms. Margaret O'Keeffe:

Thank you for speaking with me today regarding your offer to hire me into the Assistant Director of Administration role with XYZ Corporation. Regretfully, I am writing to decline your kind offer. While I was very interested in and enthusiastic about the opportunity to work for you, and become a member of your team, I have decided that the role is not the best fit for me at this point in my career.

I want to thank you again for taking the time to meet with me and for the generous employment offer. I am impressed by your company's goals, mission, and commitment to quality and service, and I wish you and your colleagues much continued success. I hope that we meet again in the future.

Best regards,
Samantha Jones

Accepting the Offer

Assuming that you, the HR person, the recruiter, and the hiring manager, are all in agreement on the terms of the offer, you can gratefully bring this process to a close, and seal the deal. If you've spoken with everyone but the hiring manager, calling her directly to let her know personally of your decision and to thank her for the offer, is a classy way to bring a personal touch to your acceptance. Thank her for the offer and be sure to say specifically and directly that you accept.

If you can't get her on the phone, leave her a polite voicemail with the same information, all the while expressing your gratitude. Explain to her that you will follow-up in writing, but of course wanted to reach out to her personally before you closed out the process more formally.

Then, in your official acceptance letter, thank the hiring manager for the offer and confirm your acceptance of the starting salary. Mention any specific terms you agreed to if they differ from the first offer, or from policy (*i.e.,* the second week of vacation they granted you in the first year of employment, or that generous signing bonus), and confirm your start date. Acknowledge any final terms of the deal that are still left hanging (completion of reference checks, drug screen results, etc.). Finally, you should close the letter by thanking her again for the opportunity.

Here is an example:

Dear Ms. Margaret O'Keeffe:

It was certainly a pleasure speaking with you this afternoon, and specifically to have the pleasure of accepting your offer to join your team at XYZ Company. Please consider this letter my formal acceptance.

I am pleased to accept your offer at a salary of $34,000 annually. As we agreed, my starting date will be May 1. I specifically wanted to thank you as well for your offer to provide me with an additional week of paid vacation (two weeks rather than one), and for the generous sign on bonus to help defray my relocation expenses.

Thank you again, Ms. O'Keeffe, for this wonderful opportunity. Please let me know if I can do anything in advance of my start date to help you. I look forward to working with you, and will see you again on May 1.

Warm regards,
Jim Williams

Summary

If you've devised a solid pre-game strategy in basketball, when the referee throws the ball up, you're ready to play. If you've done everything right, both in practice and in the first 35 minutes of the game, you should be confident in your ability to finish the game effectively.

This stage of the job search game is like the fourth quarter: fielding job offers, evaluating them carefully and thoughtfully, having meaningful discussions with the "players" involved, and then making tough but well thought out decisions. That's where you are now. At this stage in the process, your best bet is to slow down and take this one step at a time. You have to stay focused on the process, and follow it through, without skipping any details. The best way to reduce your stress in this career search process is to be prepared and practice, practice, practice. Perhaps your coaches were right all those years; nothing takes the place of good, old-fashioned hard work, which is often times just practice.

"I was competitive, a tireless worker, disciplined, and I was a leader. I knew that I had the ability to be successful in my chosen field based on my drive and ambition. Employers hired me based on those qualities as they were exemplified by having been a student athlete."

—SOFTWARE DEVELOPER
AND FORMER DIVISION I
MEN'S LACROSSE PLAYER

For all of the complexities throughout the entire job search process, the whole thing, top to bottom, can be boiled down to this: First, go get yourself a job offer. Then, evaluate, negotiate, accept or decline it. How hard was that?!?!

Career Spotlight

DOMINICK MARTINETTI is founder and President of SLAPPA, a consumer goods brand that distributes in 13 countries. Previously he has held senior marketing management positions with technology companies EMC, Documentum, Cordys and Cadence Design. Dominick graduated from Ramapo College of New Jersey with a BA in Business Administration and was a wide receiver on the Roadrunner football team. He also received his professional Masters Degree from Troy State University.

EXERCISE

RATIONALE: Although the time it takes to generate a job offer — from writing a resume to the completion of several rounds of interviews — can take months, you'll often be given only a relatively short time to evaluate, clarify, discuss, and eventually, accept or reject an offer. Unless you've had a great deal of experience in this final stage of the search the choices and options can be complex, and the time you'll be given to make this important decision will be pretty short. In such circumstances, having a tool to help you evaluate a job offer will be invaluable. You'll want to save one of the checklists provided below for use when you have an actual job offer; in the meantime, the first worksheet is for your current use, and it is intended to better familiarize you with the many factors that may come into play when that first offer does come.

Career Spotlight

ANDREW MUSSLER is currently a fireman for the New York City Fire Department where he has proudly served for over 18 years. He graduated from Adelphi University with a bachelors degree in communications, and he was a key member of their lacrosse team. Prior to becoming a fireman, he was a wholesale national sales representative for Burberry.

EXERCISE 14.1: **Job Offer**

DIRECTIONS: Evaluate each component of a job offer, and rank its overall importance to you on a scale of 0-10 (0 = no importance and 10= critically important).

JOB OFFER #1 COMPONENTS

COMPONENT	RANK
Company Size	
Growth Opportunity	
Location	
Benefits	
Retirement Plan	
Product or Service	
Reputation in the Market	
Financial Stability	
Culture/Environment	
Job Duties	
Level of Challenge	
Manager	
Travel	
Salary	
Bonus Potential	
Commission (if applicable)	
Moving Expenses	
Vacation	
Work Hours	
Ability to Work Remotely	
Commute	
Tuition Reimbursement	
Work/Life Balance	

JOB OFFER # 2 COMPONENTS

COMPONENT	RANK
Company Size	
Growth Opportunity	
Location	
Benefits	
Retirement Plan	
Product or Service	
Reputation in the Market	
Financial Stability	
Culture/Environment	
Job Duties	
Level of Challenge	
Manager	
Travel	
Salary	
Bonus Potential	
Commission (if applicable)	
Moving Expenses	
Vacation	
Work Hours	
Ability to Work Remotely	
Commute	
Tuition Reimbursement	
Work/Life Balance	

Afterword

Every time I meet with a prospective student-athlete, I reassure them that high school has prepared them for college, but inform them that college is designed to prepare them for life. Their excitement at that moment usually centers around two distinct areas: the ability to compete athletically at the collegiate level and a chance to attend one of the top institutions in the country. Often in that meeting, I find that student-athletes express interest in majors because it either sounds good, it is appealing to their parents or, for a select few, it has been their childhood dream.

Once that student-athlete enters college, things often seem to change. They might get a real taste of organic biology and discover medicine is not really the best option for their career, or struggle through accounting and abandon their dream of being a top executive at a Fortune 500 company. Many other student-athletes I work with have a hard time deciding what they would like to do with the "rest of their life," not realizing what that looks like will probably change many times during their professional life. The question now is where and how to start.

As a college student-athlete in today's world, you have spent a lot of time perfecting your sport. Think about it, many of you have been specializing since childhood. Consequently, most of you have developed a strong athletic identity and a sense of self-efficacy in your athletic abilities. Unfortunately, many of the athletes I work with fail to see how the same dedication they apply to their athletics, complemented with campus resources, meaningful experiences and a small dose of willpower can ignite the development of confidence and skills in other areas of their life. We have all seen the commercials reminding us that students who participate in intercollegiate athletics will likely become professional in something other than their sport. In less than a minute, the student featured on the television trades in their uniform for a business suit. While the message is not only accurate and necessary, it neglects to describe the career development process that you will need to undergo during your college career.

One thing that I continue to find interesting is that often, student-athletes who are powerful, strong, dedicated, and masterful in competition do not always see how their talents are a benefit in other areas in their life, especially in a work setting. The numerous transferrable skills developed through the athletic process make you, as student-athletes, desirable in most professional settings. What employer would not want to hire someone who performs well under pressure, is able to motivate a team around the same goal, and can lift more than 50 pounds? Ironically, the student-athlete who has the confidence to be the person to take the last shot on the court is the same student who lacks the confidence to apply to graduate school out of a fear of rejection.

After a decade of working in college athletics, I am aware that I am incredibly fortunate to work in a profession I love. I may face challenges and frustration, but because I have found a career where my interests are met and my talents are utilized, I can honestly say that I have yet to go to "work." My passion for educating, challenging and supporting student-athletes is actualized every day. I think this is a miracle considering that I spent four years of college wanting to be the next Oprah Winfrey! However, I was fortunate to have a network of people who were willing to point out that I was most energized when I was working as a peer mentor and orientation leader. Interestingly, I was also fortunate enough to obtain an awesome summer internship in the broadcasting field that completely solidified what I began to realize internally, I was not passionate about being Oprah. Following that summer, as a result of my network of people and a greater recognition of my own values, I finally found the confidence and freedom to be myself and pursue my goal of making a difference in the world around me—minus the broadcast studio.

That same desire to continue to find resources that make a difference is what most excites me about The Career Game Plan. The authors have taken a very intentional approach to providing student-athletes with a tool that demystifies the career development process. The Career Game Plan will make a difference in the life of a student—and not just student-athletes—who is ready to conquer the battles associated with finding a career. As a student, it is helpful for you to understand that this journey is meant to be challenging and can even sometimes be overwhelming. Similar to the athletic process, there are going to be times when you feel very confident in your ability to win and other moments when you may question your ability to be successful at all. That uncertainty is an appropriate part of the college experience. However, don't make the mistake of spending four or five years and neglect to address an integral aspect of the "rest of your life." Yes, as a college student-athlete, you have an incredibly rigorous schedule and there are factors that may prevent career exploration through coursework. It is also true that a great competitor simply finds a way to get things done, and this text has provided you with a step-by-step way to achieve your career goals.

The Career Game Plan provides a context for you to incorporate the best of who you are in your journey to find a career. Each module within this text has been specifically designed to help you identify and develop your career aspirations through activities, resources and sound guidance. Ultimately, one of your most significant goals as a student should be to move forward on the path to a career in which you have passion, interest and excitement. The Career Game Plan shows you exactly how you can transform into the professional displayed in those commercials. One of the greatest fears of many athletes is to hang up their jersey for the last time, and while that may be inevitable, this resource allows you to see first-hand that you never really hang up the skills you have acquired over your athletic career. It is this transition from sport to life that is the greatest contest, and based on my experiences with the countless student-athletes I have worked with, I am confident that you can all be champions in this endeavor.

> *Mattie White,*
> *Associate Athletic Director for Academic Services and*
> *Excellence Academy*
> *Senior Woman Administrator*
> *Indiana University*

Career Spotlight

SOPHIA TEMPLIN is currently an Account Executive at Finsbury Strategic Communications, a crisis public relations firm in New York City. She graduated from the University of Kansas with a Bachelor's of Science degree in Journalism with an emphasis in Strategic Communications. Sophia was a pitcher for the Kansas softball team.

Resources

Occupational Outlook Handbook

Indeed.com

Careerbuilder.com

Dice.com

Glassdoor.com

Idealist.com

LinkedIn.com

LinkUp.com

Monster.com

SimplyHired.com

References

Fast Facts. (2015). Retrieved from http://nces.ed.gov/fastfacts/display.asp?id=98. National Center for Education Statistics

Five Core Values — NAIA — Champions of Character. (2015). Retrieved from http://www.championsofcharacter.org/ViewArticle.dbml?DB_OEM_ID=27910& ATCLID=205367782

Gordan, I. (2014, July). Minor League Baseball Players Make Poverty-Level Wages. Retrieved February 2015, from MotherJones website: http://www.motherjones.com/politics/2014/06/ baseball-broshuis-minor-league-wage-income

Jobvite. (2015). Social Recruiting Survey Results 2014. Retrieved from http://www.jobvite.com/ wp-content/uploads/2014/10/Jobvite_SocialRecruiting_Survey2014.pdf

Probability of competing in sports beyond high school. (2015, February 15). Retrieved March 22, 2015,

from http://www.ncaa.org/about/resources/research/probability-competing-beyond-high-school

MLB average salary is $3.39M. (2013, December 18). Retrieved March 16, 2015, from Associated Press website: http://espn.go.com/mlb/story/_/id/10158314/mlb-average-salary-54-percent-339-million

NCAA Core Values. (2015). Retrieved from www.ncaa.org/about/ncaa-core-value

Number of jobs held, labor market activity, and. (2015, March 31). Retrieved April 17, 2015, from http://www.bls.gov/news.release/pdf/nlsoy.pdf

State of the American Workplace. (2015). Retrieved February 2015, from Gallup website: http://www.gallup.com/services/178514/state-american-workplace.aspx

Standard Occupational Classification. (n.d.). Retrieved June 15, 2015, from http://www.bls.gov/soc/

Index

About the Authors

Shaun Tyrance, Ph.D.

Shaun Tyrance is a licensed therapist who specializes in sport psychology. Shaun earned his Ph.D. in Counseling from the University of North Carolina at Charlotte and holds a Master's in Sport Psychology from the University of North Carolina at Greensboro. He was a four-year varsity letter winner in football at Davidson College where he played quarterback. Shaun served as an academic advisor for football at North Carolina State University, and the full-time Sport Psychology Consultant at Chip Ganassi Racing in NASCAR and the University of North Carolina at Charlotte. As a consultant, Shaun has worked with hundreds of college and professional athletes.

Nyaka NiiLampti, Ph.D.

Nyaka NiiLampti is a licensed psychologist and an Assistant Professor of Psychology at Queens University of Charlotte, where she also serves as Faculty Athletic Representative to the NCAA. She was a four-year varsity letter winner in track and field at Princeton University. She earned her Ph.D. in Counseling Psychology from Temple University, and has a Master's in Sport Psychology from the University of North Carolina-Chapel Hill. Her experiences have included teaching, clinical work, and serving in a consultative capacity in a variety of settings, including high schools, colleges and university and large sports organizations.

Career Partners, Inc.

Career Partners, Inc. has spent the last 30 years designing and delivering comprehensive career development programs and career counseling services for people at all stages of the career lifecycle, providing career assessment, training, and job search support to thousands of individuals and groups, including graduate and undergraduate students, across the U.S. and around the world.

CPSIA information can be obtained
at www.ICGtesting.com
Printed in the USA
BVHW091125031122
651025BV00004B/46

9 780692 916940